WhyAre
We Still in
^
Vietnam?

Why Are We Still in ^ Vietnam?

Edited by **Sam Brown and Len Ackland**

With an Introduction by Mayor John V. Lindsay

Vintage Books
A Division of Random House
New York

Preface

In 1968, political forces for peace almost turned this country around. But the Indochina war still rages on at an appalling human and material cost. The names have been changed—the gimmick is now "Vietnamization" instead of "pacification"—but the policy remains the same. So a book like *Why Are We Still in Vietnam?* is inevitable.

It reflects a very deep sense of frustration with the disastrous decision to fight on in Indochina. But, for the most part, the frustration has inspired not despair but a renewed sense of commitment to the cause of peace. *Why Are We Still in Vietnam?* exemplifies the quality of that commitment. From its initial chapters to its conclusion, it marshals rationales for an end to the war. It advances at least one specific alternative for a plan of withdrawal. Whether we agree with everything in the book (probably no one will), its real value lies in its reliance on rational analysis rather than slogans.

But *Why Are We Still in Vietnam?* will be nothing more than an ineffectual brief for a thesis—validated long ago by the tests of reason—unless concerned people act to turn reason into national policy. No one can now justify silent passivity on the question of war and peace. The stakes are too great. In the minds of millions of Americans, whether the war ends soon may well determine whether our system can work at all. Citizens, and especially public officials who are part of the system, have an obligation to make it work, to rebuild faith in the free processes of our democracy by using them to achieve peace.

From my perspective, the obligation to act is reinforced by a daily awareness of the war's consequences for my city and for other cities. So much of what should be done—for the poor and for the middle class, to reclaim the environment and to enhance the quality of American life—must be put off or forgotten because a fantastic proportion of our national resources is wasted on a bankrupt foreign adventure. Foremost among those irreplaceable lost resources are, as I write, more than forty-two thousand of our own men. We owe them the commitment of our talents and energies to a continuing campaign to end the war.

Whether we are senators or mayors, congressmen or citizens, we must work for peace because we care about America, about human decency and human life, and about the evolution of a foreign policy informed by a realistic and responsible internationalism.

Why Are We Still in Vietnam? may help the forces of peace finish the political job for securing peace. That is enough for any book.

John V. Lindsay,
Mayor

New York City
July 1970

Contents

Introduction

Why Are We Still in Vietnam? The United States is still fighting in Vietnam because none of us has persuaded our national leaders that the war must be stopped. We have failed to build powerful, effective organizations which tell the policy-makers: "Stop the war or you will be politically defeated." Until that is done and the war ends, all of us will continue to share responsibility for the Vietnam war.

The Vietnam war has now become "Nixon's War." The President, as chief of state, has the greatest power and most direct responsibility to reverse the tragic and misguided course of American policy in Vietnam. Unfortunately, Mr. Nixon appears to believe in the rationale for American intervention in Vietnam. It is this same rationale which is keeping us there today and which could expand the war even beyond Indochina.

While President Nixon is accountable for continuing a misconceived policy, he is not to blame for the initial American involvement in Vietnam. That involvement is rooted in the American Cold War anti-Communist ideology which, after 1947, became both an end in itself and a useful rhetorical tool for selling programs to the American people.

The liberals of the early 1960's added an aloof, mechanical rationalism to the "containment-of-Communism" doctrine which dominated American policy under the Truman and Eisenhower administrations. With an intoxicated self-assuredness and haughtiness the liberals set out to manipulate the world by "building nations" and "defending freedom." How many of us understood where we were headed when John F. Kennedy declared in his 1961 inaugural address that "we shall pay any price, bear any burden, meet any hardship, support any friend, oppose any foe, in order to assure the survival and success of liberty." "Liberty" was viewed simply as synonymous with anti-Communism.

The Vietnam war is also—increasingly since 1965—the American military's war. The military not only brought into Vietnam a frightening amount of destructive weaponry, it also introduced new criteria to measure progress: "body counts," "weapons and supplies captured," and "enemy structures destroyed." This language, with its euphemisms, was effective; American civilians began to think in military terms. War became a substitute for policy.

The Vietnam war is also Congress's war. It seems incredible now that it took Congress nine years after the first American soldier was killed in Vietnam before it even seriously debated appropriations for the war.

But, in the end, the Vietnam war is our war. Only by understanding the war ourselves and working to persuade others can we get together to bring the war to an end.

Why Are We Still in Vietnam? is not a comprehensive historical account of the United States' involvement in Vietnam. Nor is it a thorough analysis of the civil conflict within Vietnam. Rather, it is a book that focuses on the premises and consequences of the current American policy toward Vietnam and presents some thoughts on alternative policies. It is not a "neutral" book conceived in the academic abstract, but a book designed to inform persons about the real issues of the war.

Jeffrey Record and George McT. Kahin, have carefully investigated Mr. Nixon's statements and actions regarding Vietnam in order to discover just what the President's policy is and what it implies for the future. American policy toward Laos and Cambodia receives only minor attention in this volume since it would take another book to adequately cover the subject. And Vietnam is still the focal point of the now-widened Indochina war.

Policy-makers in Washington have characteristically created their plans for Vietnam in ignorance of the actual socio-political conditions in that country. D. Gareth Porter discusses how the American concept of legitimate government has little relevance to the Vietnamese.

Current administration policy rests on the false assumption that the costs of withdrawal are much greater than the costs of continuing the present course in Vietnam. Tran Van Dinh, Jerry M. Tinker and J. B. Neilands indicate the real costs to the Vietnamese people and society of the American actions in Vietnam. Although these costs began before Mr. Nixon took office, his policy promises to raise them substantially.

Next, Edmund Stillman and Robert Eisner write about the costs of the war to the American people and society: the sacrifices we are making to continue our futile and bloody involvement in Vietnam.

In the final section Senator George McGovern presents his ideas on a specific program for disengagement from Vietnam. Then Seyom Brown stresses the need for a fundamental transformation in the American world-view so that we can realistically face the last quarter of the twentieth century.

Since this book is an anthology of essays, each author does not necessarily agree with everything that is written by other authors.

The original idea for this book came from a number of individuals, many of whom were associated with the Vietnam Moratorium Committee, who saw the need for a small informative volume that would encompass key issues concerning the Vietnam war. All the profits from this book are being donated to help defray the debt left by the non-lucrative Moratorium Committee.

Special thanks go to Reuben McCornack for his hard work in coordinating the effort and to our diligent typist, Mrs. Giuseppe Paoli.

Len Ackland
Sam Brown

Washington
June 1970

WhyAre
We Still in
^
Vietnam?

Nixon's War

by Jeffrey Record

THE WAR IS NOW unmistakably Nixon's war. He allowed the golden opportunity to slip through his fingers. Early in his administration he could have ordered a swift and complete American pull-out from Vietnam and done so with relatively little lasting reaction at home. After all, he was not responsible for the mess; it was merely the most serious of many problems he inherited from Lyndon Johnson. In Mr. Nixon's own words, he was free to "blame the defeat . . . on him and come out as the peacemaker."

It is too late for that now. The President has inextricably entangled himself and his party in a war that has already toppled one President. After one and a half years in office and over ten thousand additional American deaths, there is still no light at the end of the tunnel, notwithstanding the illusion so deftly contrived by the administration that if only we don't debate the war, things will

Jeffrey Record served with the United States Agency for International Development as a psychological-operations adviser in Vietnam from April 1968 to August 1969. He is currently a Ph.D. candidate at the Johns Hopkins School of Advanced International Studies in Washington, D.C.

The first sections of this essay are based on an article written for the SAIS Review (Winter 1970), published by the Johns Hopkins School of Advanced International Studies.

fall into place and it will soon fade away. As the months pass by, one's sense of *déjà vu* increases, as with each step Mr. Nixon, like his predecessors, leads us further away from peace.

Shortly after he took office, President Nixon ruled out a "precipitous" American disengagement; he left the time schedule for disengagement undefined, and received support from many quarters. There was no great cry for peace in the vested inertia of the governmental bureaucracy. Too many careers were at stake. To the military, desperately seeking to preserve whatever honor it retained in the face of a performance that has been labeled grossly incompetent, "Cut and run" would have been the final confession of defeat. It is not easy to admit that Harvard and West Point can't cut it against a small bunch of pajama-clad peasants. Almost certainly, Mr. Nixon correctly assessed that his silent majority was in no hurry to end the war, especially if the flag was to be lowered and defense contracts cut away. Yet these political considerations should not be permitted to obscure Nixon the man, a self-proclaimed centrist who by instinct is not given to wide divergence from things as they are, however bad they may be.

Still, all of this skirts the core reality: Mr. Nixon and those around him profoundly believe in the war. The President, as he clearly indicated in his November 3, 1969, speech, has never felt the war to be a mistake. Of course, if only for political reasons, he has expressed doubts about the manner in which the Democrats handled the conflict, as well as regrets as to the scope of the American involvement he inherited. But he has never questioned the correctness of the involvement itself: that America should interpose its power in Vietnam to prevent a Communist take-over there.

Even a cursory glance at Mr. Nixon's public pronouncements on the war over the last decade and a half shows

that, if anything, he favored American intervention long
before it actually occurred. In 1953, as French power in
Indochina began to disintegrate in the face of determined
Viet Minh onslaughts, the then Vice President called for
a complete military victory.[1] A year later, when a French
collapse seemed imminent, Mr. Nixon noted that the
United States "as leader of the free world cannot afford
further retreat in Asia." He went on to say, "It is hoped
that the United States will not have to send troops there,
but if this government cannot avoid it, the Administration
must face up to the situation and dispatch forces." [2]

For the next decade Mr. Nixon remained an avid hawk,
attacking whenever he suspected the United States to be
veering from the narrow policy of military victory. He
complained that America was placing political reform
before battlefield victory in dealing with Diem.[3] In a 1965
speech he asserted, "[The war in Vietnam] means a Chinese Communist victory . . . we can never negotiate, sur-
render, [or] retreat . . . [We must] end the war by winning it in South Vietnam." [4]

The President has endorsed virtually all the arguments
of his predecessor: the obligation of fulfilling a prior commitment, the necessity of deterring international aggression, the conviction that Vietnam was a test case for wars
of national liberation, the prevention of Chinese Communist extension into Southeast Asia, the preclusion of a
"domino effect" in the surrounding states, and the desire
to maintain the credibility of America's word. These were
the vital American interests as perceived by Lyndon Johnson, "requiring" massive and direct American combat involvement in the war.[5] Mr. Nixon's firm belief in the war
rests on his conviction that the United States does indeed
have vital interests in Vietnam and must remain in that
beleaguered country as long as these interests cannot be
sustained by the South Vietnamese we support. The President believes that ours is a just cause in Vietnam. He is

continuing the war not in deference to the noisy generals and the silent majority, but because he is committed to it.

Mr. Nixon believes that America is committed to defend Vietnam. Lyndon Johnson's problem was to justify a commitment that did not yet exist; the President confronts a commitment already made. The question of prior formal obligation (the Southeast Asia Treaty Organization, the Eisenhower–Diem letters, etc.) is made irrelevant by an additional reason to stay in Vietnam: a "commitment" to the tens of thousands of Americans who have already lost their lives in that fruitless struggle. The "They-shall-not-have-died-in-vain" argument, with its clearly potent political implications, is alone enough, in the calculus of the administration, to compel continued American prosecution of the war. A new corollary to this argument is that the protection of American lives dictated the invasion of Cambodia. But there is no evidence that pouring additional American blood into Southeast Asia is in any way either effective or redemptive of those Americans who have already died.

Mr. Nixon believes—even more than Lyndon Johnson believed—that the failure to "see it through" would have disastrous consequences affecting faith in America's word. "If we simply abandon our effort in Vietnam," he said in May 1969, "the cause of peace might not survive the damage that would be done to other nations' confidence in our reliability." In fact, the daily unfolding of the Vietnam war has resulted in the loss of almost all our traditional allies. Not one major Western European nation has fully supported our effort in Vietnam.

On the question of wars of national liberation, the administration has remained generally silent. However, in November 1969, Nixon implied that an American defeat in Vietnam would spark similar violence "wherever our commitments help maintain the peace—in the Middle East, in Berlin, eventually even in the Western Hemisphere." But there is no indication that local problems in other parts of the world are going to be resolved in Vietnam.

Mr. Nixon is convinced that China is the real issue. As late as 1965, without qualification he labeled the war a contest between the United States and Peking.[6] As President, he has made similar, although more subtle, assertions. Such an interpretation ignores both the anti-Chinese struggles in Vietnamese history and the fact that no Chinese are fighting in a neighboring country where over 400,000 American troops are engaged.

The President endorses the domino theory apparently without reservation. In 1965 he prophesied[7] that if Vietnam fell, the United States would have to write off Laos, Cambodia, Burma, Thailand and Indonesia. He went so far as to predict that within five years the Pacific Ocean would become a "Red sea," and that the Americans would find themselves defending Australia against the Chinese. In his speech in November 1969, Mr. Nixon claimed that a "precipitate" American withdrawal would "without question promote recklessness in the councils of those great powers who have not yet abandoned their goals of world conquest" which would presumably lead to further conquests.

There seems to be little awareness on the part of the administration that it was precisely America's intervention which, by prolonging the war indefinitely, may be largely responsible for extending the conflict into neighboring states. The North Vietnamese–Pathet Lao offensive pushing beyond the Plaine des Jarres in Laos, the American invasion of neutral Cambodia purportedly to "cover" our "disengagement" in Vietnam, and the growing insurgency in Thailand, testify to the failure of a strong American military posture in Vietnam to "stabilize" the dominoes.

Thus the Nixon administration upholds, with different emphases but similar rhetoric, the old Johnsonian argu-

ments justifying the massive combat presence in Vietnam.
In addition, however, the President has come up with a
powerful new emphasis on an old argument, and one no
less dubious than the others. It is an argument not in support of *becoming* involved in Vietnam, but tailored to
justify *continuing* that involvement: it is the controversial
bloodbath argument.[8]

"When we assumed the burden of helping defend South
Vietnam," said the President in May 1969 before the
United Nations, "millions of South Vietnamese men,
women and children placed their trust in us. To abandon
them now would risk a massacre that would shock and
dismay everyone in the world who values human life."
According to the highest administration estimate, given by
Mr. Nixon in his April 30, 1970, speech, the number of
victims will reach "millions," although he leaves us in the
dark about the origin of that vague figure.[9]

In fact, most long and bitter civil wars are followed by
varying degrees of retribution and reprisal. However, the
projected bloodbath in Vietnam must be seen in perspective. In the first place, the argument may strike many
Americans as hastily contrived to counter liberal demands
for a fast pull-out. It also appears specious on other
grounds. Americans for five years have been subjected
nightly to rather convincing proof that Vietnam is, and
has been for a long time, a bloodbath of gigantic proportions (which has already "shocked and dismayed" most of
those who value human life) in which, by conservative estimates, a million Vietnamese have so far lost their lives.[10]
The suggestion that it is necessary to continue a *real*
massacre in order to prevent the *possibility* of future massacres seems, particularly since the My Lai murders, somewhat frail.

The notion that a Communist take-over of South Vietnam would bring on a reign of terror is made even more
mysterious by Mr. Nixon's implication that the United

States would acquiesce in such a take-over if it occurred
by peaceful and legitimate means. In May 1969 he stated,
"We are willing to agree to neutrality for South Vietnam
if that is what the South Vietnamese people freely choose
. . . We are prepared to accept *any* government in South
Vietnam that results from the free choice of the South
Vietnamese people themselves [emphasis mine]." Thus apparently the question of a bloodbath is tied not to a Communist victory but rather to the manner in which that
victory is achieved.

There is evidence that suggests a contrary conjecture.
There was no significant violent purge immediately following Ho Chi Minh's assumption of power in the North.
The ten to fifteen thousand peasants who, according to
historian Joseph Buttinger and other observers, were liqui-
dated two years later, were the victims of a land-collectivi-
zation scheme. If this figure is shocking, it should be noted
that more than one million innocent civilians in the South
have been killed, maimed or wounded as a result of the
war, particularly of the indiscriminate application of
American air power and artillery bombardment.[11] Thus
the carnage of innocent civilians alone (leaving aside the
750,000 or so combatant deaths on both sides) surpasses
most higher estimates of the numbers of those who would
be victims *if* a bloodbath did occur. Despite the much-
publicized Catholic migration to the South from 1954 to
1956 (Catholics are often cited as a prime target for liqui-
dation in the event of an enemy victory), 800,000 Catholics
still live in the North and have not been subjected to
massacre, purge, or even unusually harsh treatment. The
ethnic minorities in the North suffer less discrimination
and possess more autonomy than their kinsmen in the
South. Certainly, the harsh incarceration of political devi-
ants would be nothing new to the South Vietnamese. And
a large number of those higher officials who might be
singled out for rough treatment by Hanoi would surely

have flown to Paris or Switzerland by the time the Communists took over.

Mr. Nixon has clearly chosen to thrust the bloodbath argument before the American people as a fundamental reason for our continued large-scale presence in Vietnam for an indefinite period. Although the American public may have accepted the argument for now, time is against the administration. As the months go by, the continuing butchery in Vietnam will erode the proposition. And with the demise of its credibility will come the end of even this superficially convincing reason for continuing major American involvement in that tortured country.

It is infinitely easier to infer what the President feels about the war than to know what he intends to do about it. Despite election promises of a "plan" to "end the war and win the peace," the curtain of mystery surrounding Mr. Nixon's plan is almost as impenetrable now as it was then. The war continues unabated. No one seems to know for sure—or if he does, he isn't telling—exactly what the President's policy is. Indeed, some critics question the very existence of a coherent policy.

The two terms most closely associated with current policy—"Vietnamization" and "withdrawal"—remain ambiguous in the public mind. Vietnamization, presumably meaning the increasing assumption of South Vietnam's defense by the South Vietnamese, has never been operationally defined. Is it purely a military concept referring only to the rearmament and training of Vietnamese security forces, or does it include the reorganization and rejuvenation of Saigon politics as well? Replacement apparently means a growing American withdrawal or disengagement from South Vietnam. It, too, is a riddle. Does it mean only combat troops or the entire military presence? The President has been less than punctilious. In his November 3 address, he stated, "[We] have adopted a plan which we have worked out in cooperation with the South

Vietnamese for the complete withdrawal of all United States *ground combat* forces and their replacement by South Vietnamese forces on an orderly scheduled timetable [italics added]." Yet, a few paragraphs later in the same speech, Mr. Nixon referred to a withdrawal of "all our forces." Six months later, in his April 20 address, the President was still unclear. "I again reaffirm this government's acceptance of eventual total withdrawal of American troops," he said. Later in the speech, however, he referred only to "combat forces." This apparently means that even after Mr. Nixon's schedule is completed, some 225,-000 American troops—who are not ground combat forces —will be left in Vietnam.

There is also the contradiction between the "orderly scheduled timetable," which has already been "worked out," and the Nixon-Thieu joint communiqué issued after the Midway conference in July 1969: "Both Presidents have agreed that the replacement program should be carried out in consonance with the security situation prevailing at the moment."

The obliqueness of Mr. Nixon's policy may mask some shift from the policies of the previous administration, but the main objective of American policy in Vietnam has been remarkably consistent: the prevention of a forcible Communist take-over. This objective has usually been presented as the defense of "the right of self-determination for the people of South Vietnam" (as long, of course, as the exercise of that right would not lead to a Communist victory, as it clearly would have in 1956, when the United States opposed the free elections called for by the Geneva Conference), or the preclusion of victory for the "forces of violence." [12]

What separates Mr. Nixon from Lyndon Johnson is not the objective in Vietnam but the means. Prior to Johnson's famous speech of renunciation on March 31, 1968, military victory was the means to an end. The Tet offen-

sive, despite General Westmoreland's perception of it as a
great defeat for the enemy, did in fact deliver a decisive
blow to the American will to continue the war under an
open-ended policy of military escalation. It convinced the
Johnson administration that further pursuit of a purely
military solution was, if not impossible on the battlefield,
no longer acceptable to the American people. Johnson's
decision not to seek reelection and his search for a political
settlement reflected his awareness of the new popular
mood. Indeed, his ultimate refusal to accede to the generals' request for an additional 206,000 men (an odd request
in the light of Westmoreland's great victory) and his termination of the bombing of North Vietnam removed the possibility, if there ever was one, of a battlefield decision. Mr.
Nixon, as if to assuage fears of a resumption of the old
strategy, said, in criticism of that strategy, that it "did not
adequately stress the goal of strengthening the South Vietnamese so that they could defend themselves when we left."
In May 1969 he seemed to leave little doubt: "We have
ruled out attempting to impose a purely military solution
on the battlefield." However, the invasion of Cambodia
in late April 1970 resurrected that doubt about the President's attitude toward a military solution.

If we cannot "win" by military means, can we prevent a
Hanoi victory through other means? The Nixon policy
seems to rest upon the assumption that we can. Although
Secretary of State William Rogers has stated that the
process of Vietnamization is "irreversible," the President
has said that the policy is dependent on three vaguely
defined conditions. First, "progress" in the Paris negotiations. Unfortunately, aside from a complete capitulation by
the Communists, what constitutes progress remains a
highly guarded secret. Second, continued low level of
enemy activity on the battlefield. "If the level of enemy
activity significantly increases," noted the President in November 1969, "we might have to adjust our timetable

accordingly . . . If I conclude that increased enemy action
jeopardizes our remaining forces in Vietnam, I shall not
hesitate to take strong and effective measures to deal with
the situation." This warning has been repeated several
times since November. Such enemy action is usually taken
to mean another Tet-style offensive, intensive shelling of
major population centers, the reentry of certain North
Vietnamese regular units into the South Vietnamese struggle, or, as in the Cambodian case, a build-up of sanctuaries
(if we listen to the President) or a movement away from
the South Vietnamese border (if we listen to the Secretary
of Defense). Third, there must be adequate progress in the
Vietnamization of the war.

Some observers have concluded that the very ambiguity
of Mr. Nixon's public pronouncements reflects a desire, as
well as an ability, to remain flexible and keep his options
open. Actually the Nixon policy has exactly the opposite
effect if we are to take the President at his word. It appears
that the rate and size of American disengagement from
Vietnam will be determined not by decision-makers in
Washington but by North Vietnamese and National Liberation Front negotiators in Paris, by enemy commanders
in the field, and by the willingness and ability of Saigon to
defend itself. We seem to have completely abandoned ourselves to the actions of others. Can this be the policy of an
administration which places so much emphasis on "retain-
ing the initiative"? There is no evidence that enemy negotiators are willing to make progress in Paris, because
neither we nor the South Vietnamese are interested in making any concessions on the central subject of the talks,
namely, Who will run Saigon in the future? The President
has admitted that after two years of bargaining in Paris "no
progress has taken place on the negotiating front." Nor is
there any assurance that North Vietnamese field commanders are committed to a continuation of low posture
in the South. A fresh and well-armed North Vietnamese

army now threatens to engulf Laos completely, and the fighting in Cambodia is not likely to abate.

Thus the Paris talks and the level of enemy activity have not evolved in the direction the Nixon administration had hoped they would. Since the North Vietnamese appear to have no interest in playing the game our way, the President has discarded both progress at Paris and continued low level of enemy activity as criteria for American disengagement, leaving the entire weight of American policy wobbling on the shaky shoulders of Vietnamization alone. This was the message of the President's speech this past April 20.

It is in Vietnamization that the vulnerability—indeed, the mortality—of Mr. Nixon's policy resides. In 1954 Mr. Nixon stated that "the Vietnamese lack the ability to conduct a war by themselves or govern themselves." In 1966 he objected to President Johnson's call for mutual American and North Vietnamese withdrawals from the South on the grounds that the South Vietnamese Army would be left at the mercy of the indigenous Viet Cong.[13] Yet the implicit assumption of Vietnamization is that the ARVN (Army of the Republic of Vietnam) will be able to take on not only the Viet-Cong but also the North Vietnamese regulars.

One truth Americans should have learned in Vietnam over the past fifteen years is that "our" South Vietnamese can't, don't, and won't fight. This central reality led to American involvement in the first place. For a President, five years later, to hinge the future of America's entire policy toward Vietnam upon a client army that seems to perform best when confronted with Cambodian peasants or wounded war veterans in the streets of Saigon is an act of sheer delusion. Equipping the ARVN with modern weaponry, teaching young South Vietnamese how to fly supersonic aircraft, and training their commanders in

tactics which have not worked even when employed by
the Americans in Vietnam seem fairly hopeless as measures
to improve Saigon's effectiveness on the battlefield. It is
fantasy or, at the most, disastrous miscalculation, to assume that an American-trained and an American-supplied
South Vietnamese Army is going to carry the ball against
an enemy who has already manifested the ability to stand
off, if not defeat, the American military itself.

The real crunch is still in the future. The 115,000
Americans that Mr. Nixon withdrew from Vietnam by
April 15, 1970, represented only 20 percent of the total
American presence. Post-April 15 withdrawals are scheduled to cut deeply into our real combat strength, and it
is these cutbacks that will prove the acid test of Vietnamization. The Pentagon has already shown signs of dragging
its feet on further cutbacks, perhaps because of a growing
conviction that the ARVN cannot be relied upon to carry
the burden. Prior to Mr. Nixon's April 20 announcement
of an additional withdrawal of 150,000 men by the spring
of 1971, it was an open secret that General William Westmoreland and General Creighton Abrams were calling for
a six-month suspension of all further withdrawals. If the
situation in Vietnam or Cambodia and Laos deteriorates
(as it seems to have) to the extent that Mr. Nixon feels he
cannot keep his April pledge, he can wait until after the
1970 elections to break the harsh news to the American
public.

Walter Lippmann has summarized the ambiguity and
confusion in current Vietnam policy. "This is just about
the first time in the history of warfare that a nation thought
it could prevail by withdrawing combat troops and reducing its military presence." [14] Lippmann contends that the
Nixon administration is not seeking full disengagement at
all but is trying to "buy patience and endurance from
the American people for an indefinitely long occupation

in South Vietnam." He goes on to say that the immediate
aim of current policy is to reduce American casualties and
take the war off the front pages so that Mr. Nixon can
make an open-ended Korea-like military presence (of perhaps over 200,000 men) in South Vietnam palatable to the
American public.

Unfortunately there is little reason to doubt Mr.
Lippmann's conclusions. Secretary of Defense Melvin
Laird has already indicated there will continue to be an
indefinite presence of an American "residual" force of
advisers even after "withdrawal." Oddly enough, it was
just such a force of American advisers that helped to bring
about our tragic involvement in the first place.

NOTES

1. *New York Times,* November 8, 1953, p. 28.

2. *New York Times,* April 17, 1954, p. 13.

3. *Congressional Record,* U.S. Senate, 89th Cong., September 2, 1965, pp. 21928–30.

4. *Ibid.*

5. For a detailed analysis of the Johnson administration's justifications for America's combat intervention in Vietnam, see George McT. Kahin and John W. Lewis, *United States in Vietnam* (New York: Dial Press, 1967).

6. *Congressional Record,* U.S. Senate, 89th Cong., September 2, 1965, pp. 21928–30.

7. Theodore Draper, *The Abuse of Power* (New York: Viking, 1967), p. 116.

8. See D. Gareth Porter and Len E. Ackland, "Vietnam: The Blood-bath Argument," *Christian Century,* November 5, 1969, pp. 1414–17.

9. A RAND Corporation report (Stephen T. Hosmer, *Viet Cong Repression and Its Implications for the Future,* R-475/1-ARPA, May, 1970, p. 186) estimates that 100,000 persons would be killed in the event of a complete Communist take-over.

10. Up to June 20, 1970, the U.S. Department of Defense listed 110,162 ARVN soldiers and 652,296 enemy soldiers as killed. In addition, over 300,000 South Vietnamese civilian deaths have been recorded.

11. The massacre of civilians in Hue during the NVA/NLF occupation in the Tet offensive is often cited by the administration as an example of what would happen in Vietnam on a much larger scale were the Communists to take over. As brutal and as unnecessary as that atrocity was,

it, too, must be seen in perspective. Observers have pointed out that a far larger number of civilians were killed during the battle for Hue by Allied shelling and bombing.

12. *Department of State Bulletin*, April 26, 1965, pp. 606–10.

13. Draper, *op. cit.*, p. 147.

14. Walter Lippmann, "The Problems of Vietnam," *Newsweek*, December 1, 1969, p. 27.

The Nixon Strategy

by George McT. Kahin

RICHARD NIXON came to office recognizing that his electoral mandate was to end the war in Vietnam. Dissociated in the public's mind from his predecessor's Vietnam policy, he appeared to have broad latitude for negotiating a peace settlement. Actually, however, because of the limitations imposed by the personality and viewpoint with which he entered office, this latitude was much narrower than many assumed. He has, in fact, been strongly circumscribed by premises and assumptions very close to those of Lyndon Johnson. And this has greatly diminished his scope and flexibility for dealing with the problem of Vietnam.

His perception of the problem is not simply a matter of inheritance from the Johnson and Kennedy administrations. It must be recalled that some of their most basic premises and assumptions regarding Vietnam derived in

George McT. Kahin taught at the Johns Hopkins University from 1949 to 1950, and since 1951 has been professor of government at Cornell University, where he is director of the Southeast Asia Program. He was a member of the board of directors of the Association of Asian Studies from 1963 to 1967 and a member of the East Asia Advisory Council of the Department of State from 1967 to 1969. He wrote Nationalism and Revolution in Indonesia *and* The Asian–African Conference, *and co-authored (with John W. Lewis)* The United States in Vietnam.

large measure from the Eisenhower and Truman periods. Richard Nixon was himself part of the Dulles-Eisenhower leadership that first formulated some of those concepts so central to Kennedy's and Johnson's view of Vietnam and which helped establish the necessary political context for America's subsequent heavy military involvement. As Vice President he was not only a proponent of military intervention in Vietnam, he was also a strong and consistent supporter of John Foster Dulles' effort to establish a separate, anti-Communist state in the southern half of Vietnam in defiance of the 1954 Geneva Agreements.

Although the idea that the Vietnam war was a result of aggression from the North was developed as a rationalization for American military intervention primarily by the Kennedy and Johnson administrations, the first adumbration of this distortion of history was present during Richard Nixon's last year as Vice President. He has been quite as adamant as President Johnson in insisting that the war in Vietnam originated in an invasion by the North, rather than as a civil war generated by southerners and essentially rooted in the South. And he adheres strictly to the Kennedy–Johnson thesis that the NLF, rather than being of basically southern origin, is a creation of Hanoi, operating under Hanoi's *Diktat*.

Anyone encumbered with such premises and assumptions has his scope and options for ending the war tremendously narrowed. And without a set of new advisers with judgments unimpaired by the need to protect reputations tied to past misperceptions and mistakes, it would be difficult for any President, however open-minded, to pursue policies inconsistent with these premises. By reappointing Ambassadors Ellsworth Bunker and Henry Cabot Lodge, while at the same time relying on judgments by the same military leadership upon which his predecessor had depended, President Nixon ensured that the interpretation of developments in Vietnam and the

advice he received would tend to conform to and rein-
force the premises and biases which a priori he shares
with these men. Of the "new team" which the President
brought in on Vietnam, Henry Kissinger has evidenced
no disposition to challenge these central assumptions,
and the President has found them shared by his even more in-
fluential adviser on Vietnam policy, his close friend and
confidant Attorney General John Mitchell.

Like Johnson, Nixon has been much more concerned
with the international context of the Vietnam problem
and with its repercussions on the American political
scene than with its solution in Vietnamese terms and in
accordance with the interests of the Vietnamese. Vietnam
is regarded as an example for those other anti-Communist
states which the administration wishes to keep aligned
with the United States. For them, as for an American domestic audience, it is to be seen not only as a test of
American military power in essentially military terms,
but also as a test of whether this power can be utilized to
shape political developments abroad in conformity with
American objectives. Nixon has been quite as determined
as Johnson that the United States should not be associated
with any political formula that allowed Asian territory to
come under Communist control; and thus he believes that
South Vietnam must be maintained as a separate anti-
Communist state. And, as with President Johnson, for
President Nixon events in Vietnam must not permit the
interpretation that during his administration the United
States sustained its first military defeat.

Despite the congruence of their views on the background and contemporary context of the Vietnam war,
two related factors have set President Nixon's approach
apart from that of his predecessor. First, Nixon is aware
that he was elected by a public that wanted the war ended.
Second, he has apparently had a much greater preoccu-
pation (despite disclaimers) with being elected to a

second term, and an appreciation that it was the Vietnam war issue that ruined Johnson's chances for reelection.

President Nixon's anxiety over the congressional elections of 1970 and the Presidential election of 1972 has strongly affected his Vietnam strategy. It has clearly dominated his sense of timing, and it has also contributed to the prevalent impression that he has been more concerned with the public-relations side of the Vietnam problem than with its actual substance and a definitive solution.

The course the President has pursued in Vietnam has been strongly influenced by his decisions as to which parts of the electorate are indispensable to his election strategy and which he can afford to write off. Having decided to stick with the "Southern strategy" that he is convinced was crucial in his election, it is probably inevitable that he should find liberal support the most expendable. Within the context of a continued "Southern strategy" the major threat to Nixon is perceived as coming from the right, especially from the Wallace-ites. Therefore the President has moved to placate their views on Vietnam rather than those of the liberals within his own party and among independent voters.

President Nixon's rightward stance on the Vietnam issue reflects in part his appreciation that the Wallace-ites and others of their point of view would be among the first to attack him for policies which could be interpreted as genuine compromise with Hanoi and the NLF, or which appeared to abandon the maintenance of an anti-Communist state in South Vietnam. The potential danger of such attacks is not likely to be minimized by a man whose earlier political success was in no small measure due to his exploitation of the "soft-on-Communism" issue, and who came to the Vice Presidency with a party whose election strategy had been significantly dependent upon accusations that the Democrats had acquiesced in the loss of China to Communist control. Thus, to maintain right-

wing support, President Nixon remains dedicated to a
no-surrender-of-territory-to-Communist-control policy in
Vietnam. This policy implies continuing support of
Nguyen Van Thieu at least until the next Vietnamese
presidential election, scheduled for September 1971 under
the existing Saigon constitution. But in addition to the
right, the President must also keep a large part of the middle spectrum of public opinion with him on Vietnam. To
do so, he must convince them that he is moving steadily
away from military involvement there.

At the beginning of his administration President
Nixon's efforts to appeal simultaneously to the middle and
the right wing of American public opinion were reflected
in his emphasis on the importance of negotiations, while
at the same time he refused to moderate the U.S. negotiating posture in a way that might have permitted substantive negotiations to get started. And before moving on
the negotiating front it was evident that he was intent on
first convincing both his American and Vietnamese audi-
ences that he was proceeding from a position of firmness
and strength. He refused to acknowledge that Hanoi had
responded to President Johnson's November 1968 bombing halt of the North by any significant reduction in its
military activity in the South. (He was, for instance, quite
unwilling to attach any interpretation of peaceful intent
to Hanoi's withdrawal of twenty-two of its twenty-five
regiments from the northernmost parts of South Vietnam.)
Nixon ordered no change in President Johnson's directive
to General Creighton Abrams that "all-out pressure" be
applied on the enemy, and when, toward the end of February 1969, the Communists suddenly returned for a time to
their previous level of military activity he held them solely
responsible for the escalation.

Having established this tough stance, in the spring of
1969 the administration began to move seriously toward
the "two-track" approach advocated by Henry Kissinger.

This provided for concomitant efforts at negotiations between the United States and Hanoi, on the one hand, and between Saigon and the NLF on the other. The effort failed, in part because of the administration's unrealistic expectation that the Russians would find it in their interests to mediate, and that they would have sufficient influence on Hanoi to persuade it and the NLF to moderate their negotiating positions in favor of American objectives.

The effort was also doomed by some of the same assumptions that had militated against the success of negotiations by the Johnson administration. Prominent among these was the thesis that the NLF is the passive puppet of Hanoi, and that Hanoi would be prepared to engage in secret bilateral talks with the United States over the head of the NLF on matters directly affecting the South. The American position was also unrealistic in assuming that there was any genuine basis for compromise between the NLF and the Saigon government so long as Thieu could count upon U.S. military protection and economic support for an indefinite period into the future.

Finally, obsessed as it was with the idea of national honor, the Nixon administration suffered from a parochial lack of understanding of the enemy's viewpoint. It could not seem to appreciate that an adversary with one tenth of the U.S. population—which, by the administration's own count, had lost fifteen men for every American soldier killed—had its own national honor every bit as much engaged as that of the United States, particularly when its leaders saw the very survival of their country at stake. All this, of course, made quite unlikely the sort of concessions by the enemy which the administration regarded as "reasonable" prerequisites for what it insisted must be an "honorable" settlement for the United States.

The absence of any movement on the negotiation front made it increasingly difficult for the President to retain public confidence in his ability to bring the war to an end. Despite the announcement on June 8, 1969, of a token withdrawal of 25,000 American troops and the indication that there would be subsequent withdrawals, public opposition to his policy continued to grow. It was dramatized by the October 15 Moratorium and a Gallup poll which indicated that 57 percent of the population backed the proposal by Senator Charles Goodell for total withdrawal of American troops by the end of 1970.

In the face of this situation the President felt obliged to make a major appeal to the nation on November 3, 1969, elaborating his views on Vietnam in a way calculated to stem erosion of majority support within the middle sector of American public opinion. The President's address, framed in terms of loyalty and patriotism, was actually a desperate appeal to buy time. To an extent well beyond the hopes of his staff he did succeed, for a period at least, in defusing opposition to his Vietnam policy, and in winning back the support, or at least the neutrality, of most of this middle sector. But this tour de force did not contribute to an early end of the war. The result was a further hardening of the President's overall approach and a considerable reduction in his area of maneuver in any negotiations.

The plausibility of President Nixon's Vietnam policy as he has presented it to the public has been heavily dependent on a serious misrepresentation of basic facts regarding the United States' involvement in Vietnam. Thus, he began his address of November 3, 1969, by stating that "the fundamental issue" is "Why and how did the United States become involved in Vietnam in the first place?" His answer: "Fifteen years ago North Vietnam, with the logistical support of Communist China and the Soviet Union, launched a campaign to impose a Communist government on South Vietnam by instigating and supporting a revolution."

In fact, Ho Chi Minh's government was then in the process of *ending* a revolutionary war. In accordance with the 1954 Geneva Agreements it was observing an armistice and moving from military confrontation to a competition at the political level. Confident that he would win the elections scheduled for 1956, Ho had no need for a revolutionary war. Under the terms of the armistice he regrouped his military forces in the North and instructed his supporters in the South to begin political campaigning in preparation for the elections. If Ho had known that the elections would be blocked he would probably have refused to withdraw his forces from the South. Certainly he could hardly have been expected to carry out the military regrouping had he known that Secretary John Foster Dulles was planning to contravene the Geneva Agreements and keep Vietnam politically divided by building up an American-protected anti-Communist state in the South. Contrary to President Nixon's interpretation of this critical period of history, Ho Chi Minh did not resume military support of his southern adherents until some five years subsequent to the Geneva armistice, after heavy repression by Ngo Dinh Diem's regime had already driven many southern Vietnamese—non-Communist as well as pro-Communist—into rebellion. But the myth of "aggression from the North" is as essential to the rationale of Nixon's policies as it was to Johnson's.

President Nixon has taken equal liberties with history in developing his bloodbath thesis. This is probably his most successful argument against rapid withdrawal of American forces. In part because it harmonizes easily with deep-seated American anti-Communist sentiments, it has been particularly effective in neutralizing sectors of public opinion that had begun to show impatience and opposition toward his Vietnam policy. Previously expounded by the President in confidential sessions with a number of congressmen, his bloodbath argument became his most potent weapon in discrediting his opponents. He asserted that with the departure of the French armed forces from northern Vietnam following the 1954 Geneva armistice agreement, Ho Chi Minh's regime "murdered more than fifty thousand people and hundreds of thousands more died in slave labor camps." Again, the President's account is contrary to the historical record,* but on the basis of this "history" he warns Americans that a similar bloodbath will occur in the South if American forces are withdrawn before Thieu's government can stand on its own.

Against the backdrop of his own reconstruction of the post-Geneva period and an apocalyptic interpretation of the still very confusing situation which obtained in Hue during the Tet fighting of 1968, the President sets the stage for presenting Americans with a spurious set of alternatives. "We have," he declares, *"only two choices* open to us if we want to end the war," either "an immediate, pre-

---

* If his advisers had studied the reports of the International Control Commission, responsible under the 1954 Geneva armistice for investigating allegations of reprisal, they must have known that in the first two years following that armistice a total of 19 complaints alleging political reprisal in the North were lodged with the Commission, only one of which involved murder. During the same period, at least 214 were lodged against Diem's southern government, including several reports of massacres. When, in early 1957, Saigon refused to allow the ICC to continue its investigations in the South, the Commission had yet to investigate 35 alleged incidents of political reprisal in the North as against 1,047 in the South. However many of these allegations could have been substantiated, we do know that Diem's own minister of information reported publicly that between 1954 and 1960 the Saigon government had arrested 48,200 alleged Communists. It was in the fall of 1956, more than two years after the Geneva armistice, that violence occurred on a significant scale in the North. This was unconnected with the anti-French struggle and was not in reprisal against Vietnamese who had supported France against the Viet Minh. It resulted from a clumsy and unrealistic attempt to impose a Chinese Communist model of agrarian reorganization, and according to estimates of outside observers, between ten and fifty thousand people were killed. As a consequence, these agrarian policies were discredited and dropped, and Hanoi's minister of agriculture sacked.

cipitate withdrawal of all Americans from Vietnam without regard to the effects of that action" or the continuation of his search for a quite undefined "just peace," if possible through negotiations, but in any case through "our plan for Vietnamization."

By insisting that the only alternative to his own Vietnam policy is a precipitate withdrawal "without regard for the consequences," the President ignores a whole range of intermediate options. He lumps all his critics together as advocates of irresponsible retreat willing to countenance a shameful abandonment of those who support Saigon to violent retribution by the Communists. Thus, those who advocate a more rapid disengagement than the President desires are charged with courting a bloodbath.

It is difficult to describe what the President and his closest advisers actually believe they can ultimately accomplish in Vietnam, because they are not at all sure themselves. In fact, their policy projections are drawn up largely *in vacuo* with little realistic relationship to the Indochina context—whether with respect to Viet-Cong and Hanoi attitudes, the political balance in Laos, or that in Cambodia. As the policy has unfolded, it has become increasingly clear that apart from the objective of maintaining a non-Communist government in power in Saigon, it is a reactive policy which attempts spasmodically to attune pursuit of that objective to changing political and military factors well out of the administration's control.

But what the administration wants the public to believe is very clear. The central feature of its public approach is that under President Nixon the United States faces neither political nor military defeat in Vietnam, nor any further extensive loss of American lives there. Rather, Americans are to expect that the United States will be successful in Vietnam—both in the sense that the military situation will so improve that most U.S. troops will be brought home and few additional Americans will die there; and that a viable anti-Communist government will be left standing in Saigon, one strong enough to stave off threats from both the NLF and Hanoi.

President Nixon has described the essence of his Vietnamization policy as being the progressive replacement of American armed forces by those of the Saigon government as the expansion, training and re-arming of the latter make this possible, with the most immediate objective being the transfer of ground-combat roles from Americans to these Vietnamese. The continuing withdrawal of American troops, he says, depends upon three conditions: the degree of progress in building up and training South Vietnamese forces so that they can take over from Americans; the enemy's maintenance of a reduced level of military activity; and "progress" at the Paris talks. The President alone, of course, has the power of interpreting whether or not these conditions are being met, and more specifically whether the extent is sufficient to warrant continued withdrawal. In fact, with respect to the second proposition, during the first half of 1970 the criterion of reduced level of enemy military activity was expanded geographically beyond Vietnam and made to apply to Laos and Cambodia as well.

Vietnamization is not meant to be a peace plan. Rather, it postulates continuation of an essentially military approach to the problems of South Vietnam, albeit in a way which, the administration hopes, will be acceptable to most Americans. It is meant to relieve Americans of feelings of responsibility for the war, by appearing to shift the fighting from U.S. to South Vietnamese soldiers, even though a decisive role is actually to be played by American troops and pilots for years to come. But it is hoped that the shift in ground-combat roles from Americans to Vietnamese will be substantial enough to keep U.S. casualties down to a level that a majority of the American public will regard as "tolerable."

The vaguest and least developed of the President's three
conditions for continued withdrawal is that of "progress at
Paris," and since the summer of 1969 his policy statements
have been marked by an almost complete lack of concern
with negotiations. Indeed, if there has been any widespread agreement as to the administration's strategy, it is
that negotiations have been distinctly downgraded, a conclusion which was reinforced when, at the end of 1969,
the President refused to replace Ambassador Henry Cabot
Lodge with a man of political stature, but instead ap-
pointed a foreign service officer who had served under
earlier negotiators and had never even occupied the post
of ambassador. Since the appointment of David Bruce
on July 1, 1970, as head of the United States' Paris delegation was unaccompanied by any indication that the administration's negotiating position had changed, it was
difficult to know whether this appointment reflected a
genuine willingness to make serious efforts at negotiation
or was simply a political move aimed at countering the
adverse public reaction to the invasion of Cambodia.

Additional obstacles to negotiations are to be found in
the Nixon administration's frequent misrepresentation of
the current negotiating position of Hanoi and the NLF,*
and its increasing tendency to move back to the pre-1968
Johnsonian position of ignoring the NLF and acting as if
it is of no consequence. Nowhere in the November 3
speech is there any mention of the National Liberation
Front, and from nearly all of President Nixon's statements, as from those of Johnson in 1965, one would assume that there are only three parties to the conflict: the
United States, Saigon and Hanoi.

The element in the Nixon administration's policy which

---

* Notable among these misrepresentations is the President's charge that
Hanoi refuses even to discuss American proposals until the United States
"withdraws all American forces immediately and unconditionally," with
the United States being required to "overthrow the government of South
Vietnam as we leave."

has most effectively blocked the way to any negotiated settlement has been its unstinting support of Nguyen Van
Thieu and its insistence that any settlement through elections must be carried out under the aegis of his government. It is, of course, hardly realistic to expect the NLF
to turn in its arms prior to elections and to assume that its
members would be treated any better than those numerous
Buddhist and other non-Communist leaders who have for
so long languished on the prison island Con Son and in
Saigon's jails as political prisoners.

To those Americans who might be alienated by the
evident downgrading of the peace talks, the administration
asserts that the very process of Vietnamization will improve prospects for meaningful negotiations. It argues
that the emergence of a much more powerful South Vietnamese army will so alarm the enemy that they will soon
take a more moderate negotiating stance toward the
United States. In short, the enemy will prefer to negotiate
with Nixon now rather than with a more powerful and
intractable Saigon a year or two later. This view was
spelled out by the President in his press conference of November 9, when he stated that as the program for Vietnamization continues, "the pressures for the enemy then
to negotiate a settlement will greatly increase, for once we
are out and the South Vietnamese are there they will have
a much harder individual to negotiate with than they had
when we were there."

Further negotiation, therefore, is seen to be dependent
upon the success of Vietnamization. Actually, however, as
will be noted below, Vietnamization constitutes a major
impediment to negotiation. Moreover, the administration
is fully aware that the NLF and Hanoi are prepared to
fight a protracted war and that there are no indications
that they would feel disadvantaged by having to deal with
Saigon alone—in fact, quite the opposite is true.

President Nixon's decision to invade Cambodia has

further reduced prospects for achieving a negotiated settlement of the war in Vietnam. By enlarging the area of conflict and the scope of American commitments and by increasing the number of disputing parties, it has added enormously to the length and complexity of any agenda for negotiations. With the Americans and the Vietnamese now enmeshed in a Cambodian civil war, a complex and intractable Cambodian problem has been tied to the thus far insoluble and interrelated problems of Vietnam and Laos.

President Nixon has realized that in order to keep the majority of Americans sufficiently supportive of his administration, the reduction of American military forces in Vietnam will have to continue. On April 20, 1970, he announced that the withdrawals of 110,000 troops between June of 1969 and April 15, 1970, would be followed by the departure of an additional 150,000 from Vietnam sometime before May of 1971. With the invasion of Cambodia there was a substantial decrease in the rate of withdrawal, but the domestic political pressures and calculations bearing on the congressional elections of November 1970 induced the President to announce that one third of the 150,000 would be pulled out by October 15, 1970.

The Nixon administration's policy is clear in its insistence on sustaining an anti-Communist regime in Saigon at least through the American elections of November 1972. It is much less clear with regard to what happens thereafter. In fact, the administration's military advisers do not believe that the Saigon government will be able, at least in the foreseeable future, to stand on its own feet. They see its capacity to withstand pressures from the NLF and Hanoi as critically dependent upon a substantial continuing American military presence. When the administration speaks of having all "ground-combat troops" out of Vietnam sometime in 1971, it leaves to itself the definition of what constitutes this military category, and it has now

made clear that a sufficient number must remain to protect residual U.S. bases in Vietnam. There is, then, no real
prospect of transforming the American military role in
Vietnam from a dirty ground war to a "clean" long-dis-
tance kind where significant numbers of American soldiers
don't get killed.

The Nixon administration's publicly reiterated confidence in its Vietnamization policy indicates that the tendency to base judgments on wishful thinking did not leave
Washington when Lyndon Johnson departed for Texas.
With few exceptions the data and interpretations that
American military and civilian personnel forward to Washington from Saigon continue to conform with what the
administration wants to hear. The official position has been
that the NLF and Hanoi are today much weaker than they
were a year ago, too weak to contest an increasing domina-
tion of rural areas by the Saigon government.

Privately, however, many officers and civilian officials
admit to a considerable uneasiness as to what the enemy's
capacity and intentions actually are. They are quite unsure
whether the decreased level of the enemy's military activity has been a freely chosen course, reflecting an appreciation by Hanoi and the NLF that they are sufficiently
master of the calendar to wait and see how sustained and
substantial the American military withdrawal will be before they step up offensive action to a point which might
risk slowing the rate of that withdrawal.

Rarely do American officials stray from the official administration and U.S. Army line concerning the NLF.
Thus, by insisting that politically as well as militarily the
NLF and Hanoi are one tightly integrated monolith, they
are able to evade answering one of the really central questions arising from the administration's Vietnam strategy:
How long will it be in the interests of the NLF to accept
the current rate of American troop withdrawal? Is it realistic to expect that a revolutionary force so heavily depend-

ent upon local backing can continue to defer responding to local pressures for decisive action? Can the NLF be expected to ask its constituency to wait until President Nixon wins his election in November 1972 before it is relieved of further heavy-handed efforts at "pacification" by Saigon and the United States and before insisting that an all-out military effort is made to bring the long war to a conclusion?

In fact, then, the policy of Vietnamization has not really been tested. In South Vietnam, American combat forces still play the dominant role, and American military power continues to provide a massive shield for most of the South Vietnamese armed forces. At least until the invasion of Cambodia, something like a period of reprieve was in effect while the enemy tried to fathom President Nixon's intentions and gauge the benefit of American troop withdrawals. But, of course, the administration cannot know what constitutes the minimum pace of American disengagement sufficient to provide continuing inducement to the NLF and Hanoi to maintain a reduced level of fighting. Nor can it know what other considerations relevant to their interests might outweigh this advantage.

What is officially described as Vietnamization does not, of course, cover all the changes in American military deployment undertaken by the Nixon administration. While there has been a reduction in the areas of South Vietnam where American forces are regularly involved (especially within the delta, the central highlands and the interior of the northern provinces), there has been no such diminution in the area subjected to American air strikes. Withdrawal from territory has not meant abandoning it to the enemy. Raids by B-52's and other aircraft, together with harassment and interdiction artillery barrages, are relied upon to deny much of this territory to the NLF, or at least to drive out so much of the peasantry as to reduce greatly the population base from which it can recruit military manpower.

In Laos both the weight and extent of American strategic and tactical air activity have considerably increased. In addition, in September 1969, American-financed-and-directed Laotian forces (largely Meo tribesmen) pushed much further east into previously Communist-dominated areas of the country. The powerful riposte made by North Vietnamese forces in early 1970, driving the U.S.-supported Laotian troops back far beyond the point from which they launched their attack, demonstrated not merely the ineffectiveness of the increased American military involvement in Laos; it also exposed the fragility of Vietnamization. Clearly if Hanoi can so rapidly augment its military forces in Laos, it can do the same in South Vietnam—or in Cambodia—whenever the time seems most propitious.

The most dramatic revelation of the failing prospects of the President's Vietnamization policy came at the end of April 1970, when he astonished most of his own closest advisers with his precipitate decision to extend military operations into Cambodia. The success of his Vietnamization policy and the continuing withdrawal of American troops, he argued, required this expansion of the war. The move was suddenly deemed essential, even though neither his nor Johnson's administration had ever previously regarded the Vietnamese Communists' Cambodian border bases as of sufficient importance to warrant mounting a major invasion to eradicate them. If, with the impending departure of additional American troops from South Vietnam, these same bases now posed a critical threat to the Vietnamization program, the conclusion was inescapable that this program was not proving successful. In short, it was not producing the augmentation in strength of Saigon's forces sufficient to compensate for the promised reduction of American manpower in Vietnam.

Very possibly President Nixon's most important reason for ordering the invasion of Cambodia was the expectation that this would shore up the tottering Phnom Penh regime led by Lon Nol. But an intervention with this objective was so patiently inconsistent with the Nixon doctrine of eschewing new commitments that the President could not afford to announce it publicly. Thus the official rationale for the invasion of Cambodia was limited to protecting the process of Vietnamization and ensuring the continuing withdrawal of American troops from Vietnam.

Once having unleashed the South Vietnamese army, President Nixon has been unwilling to restrain Saigon from attempting a long-term occupation of large areas of Cambodia for purposes quite unrelated to the original announced American objective of destroying the Communist border bases. With the South Vietnamese insisting that their object is to maintain sufficient military forces in Cambodia to keep General Lon Nol's narrowly based government in power, prospects for the United States' disengagement from Vietnam have increasingly become a hostage of political developments in Cambodia. A South Vietnamese government which cannot stand by itself without massive American support is now engaged in propping up an equally unrepresentative Cambodian regime that could never be viable on its own. Politically as well as militarily, U.S. power has been extended both directly and indirectly into Cambodia. Even if American air power and advisers, as well as American ground troops, should be completely and permanently withdrawn from that country, the United States will, in a major sense, still be involved by proxy through the firepower of Saigon's troops whose absence from South Vietnam can only be offset by the compensating presence there of American forces.

Thus the scope of the war has been greatly expanded without any significant change in the balance of military power. The South Vietnamese army, whose capacity to defend even South Vietnam remains critically dependent upon American military manpower, is now called upon to spread its resources ever more thinly in long-term ground operations over much of Cambodia. Consequently the number of Vietnamese soldiers available to relieve Americans in Vietnam has been drastically reduced. To extend assignment of South Vietnamese forces to wide areas of Cambodia makes a travesty of whatever prospects for success Vietnamization might have encountered had the role of Saigon's troops been confined to Vietnam.

The Cambodian invasion has raised serious questions which responsible American military and civilian officials have not yet answered. How can the South Vietnamese army spare the diversion of substantial numbers of its elite Khmer Krom troops (men recruited from South Vietnam's own large Cambodian minority and trained and directed by the U.S. Special Forces) for the long-term commitment in Cambodia that is already well underway? How can other South Vietnamese forces be spared to take over the roles of these and other Khmer Krom forces in the central highlands and the western delta area? How long will it remain in the interests of the Viet-Cong and Hanoi to deploy additional troops in Cambodia and Laos rather than concentrating them for major offensives in South Vietnam? Were American officials correct in welcoming the Lon Nol coup and assuming that American interests in Cambodia would be better served by a right-wing regime than by the neutralist leadership of Prince Norodom Sihanouk?

Some of the answers will undoubtedly depend upon Sihanouk's success in rallying support among his own peasantry and disaffected military units. With a nationalist appeal and a rapport with the peasantry that dwarfs that of Lon Nol and his lieutenants, Sihanouk's prospects in the developing civil war are considerable. Whether, once forced into dependence on the Vietnamese Communists,

Sihanouk will be able to disengage fully is by no means clear. But because of his superior nationalist credentials and popular backing, in the long run he is likely to be less dependent upon the military support of the NLF and Hanoi than Lon Nol will be upon the direct support of Saigon and Bangkok and the indirect support of Washington.

Whatever the military prospects of President Nixon's Vietnamization policy, its political impact in Vietnam is already clearly manifest. Vietnamization affects both the character of South Vietnamese politics and prospects for a peaceful settlement. It maintains in power in Saigon an unrepresentative government which is obstinately set against making any genuine effort to negotiate a political solution to the war.

The Nixon administration's unflagging support of Thieu's leadership and its dogmatic discouragement of all other non-Communist elements have served to bring about an even greater degree of political polarization in South Vietnam than obtained during the Johnson administration. This strengthening of Thieu has in general had little effect on the NLF, but it has decidedly undermined Thieu's non-Communist opposition. The increase of Saigon's army and police force called for under the Vietnamization program has made it possible for Thieu to exercise even tighter political controls, permitting him to intimidate and silence the non-Communist critics of his government more effectively than it ever did in the past.*

Thieu's increasing repression of deviant political sen-

* The increase in the number of Thieu's armed forces has been fully reported, but little has been made public concerning the tremendous increase of his national police force now underway. From a body numbering 16,000 in 1963 it reached 78,000 by the end of 1969, and is scheduled to increase to 122,000 by the end of 1970. So high is the priority assigned to this expansion of the police force that last year President Thieu transferred 13,000 men from the army to the national police.

timent has had the greatest significance for the United States. For those who are jailed or otherwise silenced tend to be those most anxious to end the fighting and to explore possibilities of a negotiated settlement with the NLF. The path to political compromise which is prerequisite to an end to the fighting is blocked, and the only way open is the old one of continuing effort toward military supremacy —that will-o'-the-wisp that is supposed ultimately to make possible negotiations from a position of greater strength.

By providing President Thieu with the assurance of continuing, even if reduced, American military support, the United States relieves him of the necessity of political accommodation in terms of the actual balance of indigenous political forces in Vietnam. Manifestly, a continuing major American military presence allied to one Vietnamese faction effectively rules out any genuine possibility for political self-determination among the Vietnamese themselves. Maintenance of the American-supported political polarization of South Vietnam ensures that those non-Communist Vietnamese most committed to a negotiated peace settlement are deprived of the possibility of working toward it.

President Nixon's Vietnam strategy is clearly more attuned to the exigencies of American domestic politics than to Vietnamese realities. He has for the time being blunted the major thrust of domestic criticism and bought time with the American public. But he has done so at the cost of rigidifying his position and narrowing his alternatives. The arguments he has employed to secure public support have shrunk the area of possible compromise with his Vietnamese opponents; and such an area is, of course, fundamental to the achievement of any negotiated peace settlement. So long as one of President Nixon's central aims is to use American military power to maintain an anti-Communist government in Saigon, he makes a mockery of any commitment to Vietnamese self-determination and thus of any real possibility for ending the war. Even if his Vietnamization strategy does lead to a significant reduction in the number of American soldiers in Vietnam, many will be required to remain and fight if that objective is to be maintained. Nixon's policy is not compatible with ending the war and, in fact, lays the basis for its indefinite prolongation.

Crisis of Legitimacy

by D. Gareth Porter

I

Despite a long period of relative "stability," the military regime in Saigon still faces a political crisis which could ultimately lead to its collapse. That political crisis is fundamentally a crisis of legitimacy characterized by a general contempt for the government at all levels of Vietnamese society.

It is not a problem which can be manipulated by American bureaucrats, even with the vast resources at their disposal. The instruments of legitimization in Western politics—a liberal constitution, elections and a national assembly—cannot alone have a substantial impact on the underlying Vietnamese attitudes toward the Saigon regime. Those attitudes have been shaped by Vietnamese culture and history, especially the profound experience of anticolonial and anti-feudal revolution, which impel Vietnamese to deny the legitimacy of the Saigon regime.

Traditionally Vietnamese judged the legitimacy of a gov-

D. Gareth Porter was an accredited correspondent in Vietnam in 1968 and is now a specialist in Vietnamese politics in the Southeast Asia Program at Cornell University. He has written for The New Republic, The Nation, Commonweal, and The Christian Century.

ernment in terms of the Confucian concept of the "mandate of Heaven," which the emperor was presumed to possess as long as he practiced the principles of goodness and justice outlined by Confucius and his disciples. If the emperor departed from those principles, it was assumed that he would lose the mandate and would be overthrown by a popular revolt. French colonialism confused the question of legitimacy by replacing the emperor with a power which was not bound by the will of Heaven. But the Viet Minh revolution of 1945 gave the traditional concept of the Heavenly mandate new vigor, even if Emperor Bao Dai, by his abdication to Ho Chi Minh's Democratic Republic, ceased to be its focus.

In the context of Vietnam's Confucian ethics and politics, the Viet Minh movement was able to hold the allegiance of most Vietnamese, even in the face of a rival French-supported government under the ex-Emperor, because its leaders and representatives more closely approximated in their conduct that virtuous government which had in the past held the mandate of Heaven. The Viet Minh never ceased to depict the struggle as one in which their moral superiority was pitted against the superior physical power of the French. As Truong Chinh formulated it, "most of the enemy's weaknesses are of a moral nature. As for us, our weaknesses are for the most part material and our strong points moral." [1]

The contrast between the austerity and self-sacrifice associated with Ho Chi Minh, the son of a poor scholar, and the greed and self-indulgence of Bao Dai and the men around him symbolized the moral distinction between the two rival claimants to legitimacy.[2] Both the redistribution of power in the countryside and the drive to liberate the country from a foreign oppressor were perceived by Vietnamese as a return to the proper Confucian principles of society, a sweeping away of those who had risen to power and wealth under the French, and thus a real *cach mang,* or "changing of the mandate," which is the only Vietnamese term for revolution. In a real sense, the countryside, which still believed in the Confucian virtues in government, was asserting its ethic over an urbanized and Westernized elite which had forgotten the traditional basis of legitimate government.

If one term can sum up the Viet Minh's moral basis of legitimacy, severed from this institution of the emperor, it is the term *chinh nghia,* meaning "just cause" or simply "righteousness." It is no accident that the political rivals of the Communists have tried to appropriate this term and to invoke the values which have been popularly associated with it in the postcolonial period. For the Viet Minh revolution undoubtedly imposed its standards of legitimacy on South Vietnamese politics, even after the enforced division of the country into Viet Minh and "pro-Western" zones.

Thus the military leadership which has held the reins of power in South Vietnam since 1965 has embraced the language of nationalism, social revolution and the renunciation of self-interest. When Premier Nguyen Cao Ky proclaimed his government to be the "government of the poor" and heaped scorn on the "minority who live in the cities . . . eat European food and drive in American cars," [3] he was invoking the spirit of rural Vietnamese political values. The Deputy Premier, General Nguyen Huu Co, in proclaiming the primacy for the army of "serving the right cause" over offering material goods, was merely recognizing the crucial importance of *chinh nghia* to political legitimacy. [4]

Yet the military leaders have never been able to achieve that legitimacy because of the origins and character of the South Vietnamese military leadership as well as its relationship with the United States. The judgment of Doan Thanh Liem, a young lawyer much admired by Americans for his community organization work in Saigon, is representative: "Leadership spawned by the American period

has largely been military, not only unnatural in the course
of Vietnamese history, but also of quite spurious origins.
The military establishment which now rules has neither
the respect nor the confidence of a large enough segment
of the population to do so for an extended period." [5]

The very idea of government by military men makes
most Vietnamese uneasy, as Liem's reference to its "unnatural character" reminds us. Even more important than
this Confucian cultural prejudice against the military men
is the view that military rule in Vietnam has "spurious
origins." The predominant belief is that the military
could not have risen and remained there without the
sponsorship and protection of the Americans.

The officer corps was, after all, not a symbol of national
liberation but a creation of French colonialism in its attempt to bolster Bao Dai's regime. The negative attitude
toward officers of the Bao Dai army during the postcolonial
period is illustrated by an ARVN (Army of the Republic
of Vietnam) troop-indoctrination booklet published in
1956. This booklet accused the pre-1954 army of having
been "mercenaries for the colonialists," and said that the
army had lost both "the just cause" and the "confidence
and support of the people." [6]

Although Diem promised a "new Republican Army,"
the fact is that all of the officers who held high positions
under Diem and after—including President Thieu, Vice
President Ky and Premier Khiem—served as officers in the
colonial Vietnamese Army or were trained by the French
military. As one Saigon editor said in 1968, "People simply
have no trust in Thieu and Ky, who worked for the French
and thus have risen high by treason." [7]

If the colonial origins of the military leaders have made
Vietnamese skeptical of their nationalist credentials, their
unconcealed dependence on the American military presence has decided the question of legitimacy for most Vietnamese. The arrival of American combat troops in 1965,

although it provoked no open demonstration of opposition for several months, nevertheless had a major impact on the political consciousness of the South Vietnamese. Those who had been subject to the influence of the National Liberation Front had long since identified the Saigon regime, whether led by Diem or his successors, as dependent on the Americans, but there were also large rural areas as well as urban strata for which the American military occupation was decisive in locating the "just cause" in the Vietnamese conflict. As a high school teacher, commenting on the Vietnamese conception of the virtuous governor, put it, "If he brings foreign armed forces into a national conflict, he is considered unrighteous." [8]

The Buddhist Struggle Movement of 1966 was more than anything else a manifestation of the widespread feeling that Vietnam, under the leadership of the military junta, had lost to the Americans the power to determine its own fate. After the repression of the Struggle Movement in Hue and Danang, with South Vietnamese troops transported from Saigon by American planes, few Vietnamese any longer doubted that it was the Americans who were in control of Vietnamese politics.[9] So obvious, in fact, was the subservience of the Saigon government to the Americans, and so patent the complete lack of popular respect for it, that it was widely assumed among Vietnamese that the Americans desired precisely such a weak, unpopular regime to further their own interests.[10]

Eighty years of French colonialism had taught the Vietnamese to assume that Westerners were in their country only to serve their *own* interests. At the end of 1967 an official U.S. survey of attitudes in the provinces revealed what its authors called a "strange drift from reality regarding the U.S. role in Vietnam." In the III Corps area, a group of middle-aged citizens were reported to believe that the mobilization law had been enacted by order of the Americans, whose aim was "the extermination of as many Vietnamese as possible." In the Mekong Delta region, educated Vietnamese were reportedly convinced that the United States was prolonging the war in its own economic self-interest.[11]

In the atmosphere of this response to the American intervention, peasants, Buddhist monks, students and intellectuals who wished to join the "just cause" had to resist the Americans and those who collaborated with them. As militant Buddhist leader Thich Tri Quang said privately in 1967, "If I am not anti-American, I will lose the good cause, the right cause."[12] The only effective resistance, of course, was that of the National Liberation Front, and many of the leaders of the Struggle Movement of 1966 later joined with the Front, as did succeeding groups of student leaders. Undoubtedly many non-Communist individuals committed themselves to the Front as the only way of saving their country from a destructive foreign influence.

The popular perception of the military leaders as lacking the "just cause" was further strengthened by the reputation of the officer corps as the most corrupt group in Vietnamese society. It is a system of corruption whose source lies at the top of the military hierarchy, where higher-ranking officers normally sell the positions of province and district chief, division and battalion commander.[13]

The same top officers are widely known to have secured lucrative sources of income from their positions, usually through the financial dealings of their wives. The most profitable endeavors naturally involve the American presence, as in the well-known case of General Cao Van Vien, the ARVN Chief of Staff for the past four years, whose wife has extensive landholdings in the resort town of Vung Tau and around the U.S. air base at Bien Hoa, on which she has constructed buildings which are rented to Americans for a profit of several thousand dollars each month.[14]

In Vietnamese political culture, this pervasive corruption signifies not only that the military leaders are personally weak and unworthy of respect, but that the government itself, no matter how "stable" it might appear, has no confidence in itself and is unlikely to be permanent. The miltary leadership's personal corruption and its dependence on a foreign presence are thus perceived as complementary characteristics of a regime whose survival is linked with the American occupation.

II

As the process of "Vietnamization" puts more and more military power and technology into the hands of the Thieu regime, Saigon's political crisis may be understood in terms of the disparity between its physical assets and its moral power. The "just cause" which the military leadership long ago lost cannot be regained by increasing ARVN manpower or firepower, any more than the NLF's "just cause" could be weakened by reducing the population base of the NLF zone through constant artillery and air bombardment and resettlement.

The most fundamental and consistent reality of the conflict, in fact, has been the contrast between the determination and confidence of the National Liberation Front and the confusion and doubt of Saigon. The latter's weakness of spirit is manifested by the general desire for an immediate end to the war within the Saigon-controlled population, apathy and confusion among Saigon's soldiers, rising opposition within the intelligentsia, and even nagging self-doubts on the part of the political leadership itself.

The 1967 presidential election campaign, far from increasing the legitimacy of Generals Thieu and Ky, merely raised popular hopes of getting rid of the military government and replacing it with a government which would negotiate an end to the war. In the Mekong Delta province of Go Cong, for example, one province official declared privately that the majority of Vietnamese wanted a civilian government in power in the hope that negotiations could, in his words, "end this fratricidal war at any price." [15]

Although in most provinces the vote was marked by manipulation and fraud, there were some provinces in which this sentiment for a negotiated peace was actually reflected in the voting results. This was true in Tay Ninh province, the home of the "Holy See" of the Cao Dai religious sect, long considered one of the groups in Vietnam firmly committed to an anti-Communist government. Because of the province chief, Colonel Ho Duc Trung, a Cao Daist who had at one time been allied with the Viet Minh against the French, the election was substantially more honest in Tay Ninh than in most other provinces, according to both U.S. and Vietnamese officials there.[16] The result was that peace candidate Truong Dinh Dzu, whose white-dove symbol became widely known in the provinces even though he himself was not, defeated the military ticket in this province, forty thousand votes to thirty thousand.

Doubts about the righteousness of the Saigon regime have deeply affected the morale of the Saigon army as well. More than anything else, the difference between the two Vietnamese armies is a matter of motivation. The NLF soldier, draftee or recruit, acquires from the Front a set of ideas about his role which are congruent with his basic political values, and he usually regards the Front as the side of patriotism and virtue—even though he may decide that he is unwilling to endure the hardships which it demands.[17] The ARVN soldier, by contrast, is likely to view his service in the Saigon army in an ambivalent and confused way. As one senior civil servant has asked, "How can we ask our privates and corporals to die for corrupt colonels and generals?" [18]

The differences in motivation and morale between the two armies were dramatically illustrated during the 1968 Tet offensive. Whereas urban dwellers all over South Vietnam complained bitterly about the unrestrained looting of their homes by ARVN soldiers often accompanied by their officers, they were unanimous in their testimony that the NLF soldiers who occupied parts of the cities for varying periods took nothing without paying. The total absence of any connection in the minds of ARVN soldiers between military service and a political ideal is indicated by the response which they were reported to have made to people who protested their looting: "After all, you don't expect us to give our lives for nothing, do you?" [19]

The draft evasion and desertion which have plagued the Saigon army for years are generally due to the reluctance of Vietnamese youth to fight for a government for which they have no respect. Although official statistics on the rate of desertions from ARVN are not likely to reflect the full extent of the problem, it appears on the basis of past performance that some 120,000 soldiers will desert this year.[20] There are so many deserters, in fact, that the government cannot possibly prosecute them; instead, they are simply sent back to military training centers after they are caught.

These training centers also receive thousands of youth who have tried to avoid the army. At the ARVN training camp in Nui Dat, it was reported last summer that more than half the men being trained were ex-draft dodgers, and the officers so feared mass desertions from the camp that no field operations were conducted.[21] Some ARVN divisions, such as the 5th Division near Saigon, are considered particularly "desertion-prone"; on the basis of their past records, about half the men assigned to the 5th are considered likely to desert.[22]

Another aspect of the political weakness of the Saigon regime is the disintegration of its base of support within the urban intelligentsia: the professors and students, editors and journalists, lawyers and other professionals whose education and career interests make them partial to bourgeois democracy and opposed to a highly disciplined structure in which peasant cadres play a vital role. These intellectuals, who have not escaped the strong currents of revolution and nationalism which have swept across Vietnam for more than a generation, are torn by conflicts of values, for their personal interests are at odds with their identification as Vietnamese.

While the Front often receives grudging respect for its nationalism and disinterestedness, the Saigon government has no claim on loyalty from the Vietnamese intellectuals. The luster of the "modern" values once associated with the West has faded as the physical destruction and social dislocation caused by the American military occupation have awakened many Vietnamese to the threat which an advanced technological power with unlimited wealth poses to their society. As one young anti-Communist journalist, watching a display of American air power, commented, "I can't help feeling that all America represents here is materialism and that the other side represents spirit. And somehow I must believe that the spirit must win." [23]

The 1967 presidential election, which was generally perceived to have been rigged, with American acquiescence, forced many students and intellectuals into active resistance against the Saigon regime. After the election the presidents of the executive committees of the student organizations at Saigon's Van Hanh and Can Tho universities said openly for the first time that U.S. intervention in Vietnamese politics had "led the Vietnamese people to believe that the Americans are replacing the French Colonialists." [24] Students who led antigovernment demonstrations and were inducted into the army, later escaped to join the Front. Well-known intellectuals, including the former director of Saigon's primary school system, slipped out of Saigon during and after the Tet offensive to join the Alliance of National Democratic and Peace Forces, which aligned itself with the Front in order to oppose the Americans.

In 1969 a significant segment of the intelligentsia formed the first legal opposition to the military regime. The Progressive Nationalist Force, which surfaced in June 1969, called for the replacement of Thieu's government by a "provisional government of national reconciliation" which would bring an end to the war through negotiations (a formula which the new Provisional Revolutionary Government, founded by the Front in June 1969, found acceptable). The manifesto issued by the Force made it clear that it rejected the military leadership as an expression of American influence in Vietnam, emphasizing that "Vietnamese are losing the right to determine their own destiny." [25] Among the fifty intellectuals, businessmen and labor leaders who joined the Force within a few weeks of its establishment were a Catholic pharmacist, the financial director of a cement factory, a representative of a bank employees' union, and two Buddhist members of the House of Representatives. [26]

Another common response among intellectuals whose occupations involve close association with the Saigon government has been to avoid overt dissent but simply to make partial and private accommodations with the Front. The best-known case is that of Nguyen Lau, the publisher of Saigon's leading English-language newspaper, the Saigon *Daily News*. Lau, who comes from a wealthy family and was educated at Oxford and the Sorbonne, is typical of many Western-educated intellectuals who are strongly anti-Communist. Last year he was arrested for having had repeated contacts with a North Vietnamese intelligence agent whom he had known in childhood. He had given the agent political information and a press card to get around Saigon with a minimum of difficulty at police checkpoints.

Although he continued to profess opposition to Communism as an "alien doctrine," Lau confessed after his arrest that he viewed Vietnam as a nation that would "live thousands of years more," and that Communism seemed to him only a "temporary nightmare" which had "no sustaining force to cause our national destruction." [27] Like many other intellectuals, Lau could not continue to actively oppose "Communism" when it was obvious that the anti-Communist side had lost the "just cause."

Even those who remain committed to actively opposing the Front cannot help feeling their cause is fatally tainted by association with the Americans. At a political meeting early in 1969, a well-known intellectual said he would appeal to religious organizations to demand the withdrawal of U.S. troops because their presence had "caused the loss of our moral rightness in fighting Communist aggression." [28]

Thus the educated urban elite, one of the few sources of political support for the Saigon regime before the open American military intervention, can no longer be counted on by Thieu. Whether or not these intellectuals collaborate with the Front, their identification with Vietnam's national integrity is far more important than their identification with the liberal values of the West.

The same traditional values which underlie the Saigon regime's crisis of legitimacy have also had a profound influence on the thinking of the military leaders themselves. The disparity between the ideals of national self-determination—and personal disinterestedness—and the realities of humiliating dependence on foreigners and widespread corruption, has created deep doubts in their minds concerning their own political power.

The earlier phase of their careers, during which they served under the French, had been a source of feelings of guilt and inferiority for many officers. The chief of the South Vietnamese Army's psychological warfare section admitted after the Geneva Conference, "We have never rid ourselves of a secret guilt complex—the complex of fighting on the side of a colonial power against the army of liberation." [29] If the passage of time had enabled these veterans of the French period to suppress their doubts, the arrival of U.S. troops once again brought into question their claim to be genuine nationalists.

For many of these officers, the American intervention, symbolizing as it did the political inferiority of the Saigon regime to the National Liberation Front, which was not under foreign control, was a demoralizing blow which began an inner disengagement from the governmental enterprise. With the realization that they did not have sufficient popular support to survive on their own, and that ultimate power over their nation was no longer in their hands, they abandoned the pretense of disinterestedness and reverted to maximization of their own interest and that of their families.

An anonymous statement by a former high military officer and government official, published in 1968, gives us an unusual insight into this response. "Nobody knows when the war will end," he wrote. "The destiny of our country will be decided by the U.S. and the great powers. The Vietnamese people are too divided. The government and the administration of today are very weak. In this tumultuous situation, it's every man for himself. Strong people quickly take advantage of their strength." [30]

This statement expressed the sense of disintegration which had been felt by many within the government. Even the more optimistic among the military leaders, however, have been plagued by nagging doubts as to the legitimacy of the regime. Vice President Nguyen Cao Ky, who has expressed himself more candidly than other military leaders, has frequently indicated, if only unintentionally, his anxiety about the righteousness of his cause.

In a 1968 interview, Ky said he "did not want people outside Vietnam to look on the military as a bunch of selfish bandits." [31] He also insisted in a talk to Saigon high school students: "The Armed Forces do not fight as mercenaries for the colonialists and foreigners." [32] His argument was that if they did fight as mercenaries, they would be receiving "high salaries and a high standard of living." The audience, however, was most likely thinking of the graft and corruption which give army officers comfortable incomes despite modest salaries. Again, last year he told reporters, "We don't want people to believe that we are puppets of the Americans." [33] His eagerness to deny that he and his colleagues are opportunists and dependents of the Americans betrays his own fear that such charges have more than a little plausibility.

Even Thieu's information minister, whose job it is to put the best face possible on his government's claim to legitimacy, revealed in a speech in the spring of 1968 his fear that the regime did appear to be subordinate to the Americans, and that the Americans in turn could be considered imperialists in Vietnam. If only a "sound anti-Communist system" could be created in South Vietnam, he said rather wistfully, the United States could no longer fear being "imperialists," while the South Vietnamese government would no longer fear that the United States would be "our boss." [34]

Despite their militant anti-Communism, therefore, the military leaders cannot help thinking in terms of the very criteria of legitimacy which have doomed them to attempting to govern without popular respect. Most of them do not have any hope that their position will improve in the foreseeable future. One of the top generals in the government, for example, virtually wrote off his generation of leaders when he said privately in 1967 that it would take another generation before Saigon could compete with the

Communists.[35] During the present period the generals know that they can only survive with American protection.

Thus President Thieu's political strategy has had two major preoccupations: slowing the rate of American withdrawal from Vietnam, and establishing a firm grip over the apparatus of political control. Ever since American domestic pressures forced President Nixon to begin the process of Vietnamization of the war, Thieu has done everything he could to delay the process and to prevent it from going too far.

Thieu made it clear in a series of statements in the fall of 1969 that he expects American troops to stay indefinitely. "The replacement of troops is not a one-year problem," Thieu said at a news conference in September. "It is a problem that will take years and years." [36] A week later he again referred to replacing U.S. forces "over a period of years," and when the interviewer noted that the phrase scared Americans, Thieu replied, "As long as we are not capable of doing this by ourselves, you must remain to help us." [37]

Thieu's primary concern with maintaining sufficient American military and political support merely underlines his dependent status to Vietnamese observers. The revelations of the My Lai massacre brought from Thieu an immediate denial that anything significant had happened, indicating clearly the priority of relations with the U.S. government and public over internal Vietnamese considerations. The Vietnamese responded with expressions of disgust, and for the first time Senator Tran Van Don, formerly chief of staff and defense minister, who is now eager to dissociate himself from the Thieu regime, was able to attack Thieu openly as a "valet of the Americans, who are his sole support." [38]

Thieu is now keenly aware that the time is long past when he can regain any legitimacy by well-planned gestures. The one point on which the U.S. mission, the Thieu regime and its opponents now agree, in fact, is that it is no longer possible for Thieu to "broaden the base" of his government.[39] If Thieu has finally agreed to support a land-reform program, it is not because he expects a decisive increase in legitimacy, but because the Americans have long been pressing him to support it.

The domestic part of Thieu's political strategy has been concentrated not on attempting to change Vietnamese attitudes but on tightening his hold over the governmental machinery. It has long been evident that his political study closely resembles that of the late President Ngo Dinh Diem, whose regime he helped to overthrow in 1963.[40] Commander of one of Diem's key anti-coup divisions, Thieu sat on the Central Committee of the secret Can Lao party, which insured loyalty to Diem in all institutions which it infiltrated, including the army. Thus he knows the techniques of suppressing opposition as well as anyone.

There have been persistent reports, emanating from the presidential palace, that Thieu is now working to build a new cadre organization along lines similar to the old Can Lao, based on the civil service, the Revolutionary Development cadres and especially the Army.[41] With an eye to the presidential election scheduled for 1971, Thieu is clearly interested in the armed forces, which now represent more than one million votes. He has been reported considering a plan under which the allegiance of the People's Self-Defense Forces, which now serve without pay, would be secured by paying selected members.[42]

Such a Diemist-style political apparatus, based on a combination of monetary rewards and coercion, offers no solution to Thieu's fundamental political crisis. It may insure that he is not overthrown from within, but it could not survive a real American disengagement—one that would no longer protect the regime from the consequences of its own illegitimacy. At the first sign of real adversity it would dissolve. Thieu has presumably not forgotten that the high officers in Diem's Can Lao party turned against that dictator when American support for President Diem began to waver.

Given the irreversible nature of its lack of legitimacy, the Thieu regime's fate will continue to depend on Nixon's increasingly fragile policy of insuring the survival of a "friendly" government. Thus, as the crisis of legitimacy confronts "Vietnamization," time is running against Thieu and his military colleagues.

NOTES

1. Dang Xuan Khu (Truong Chinh), *The Resistance Will Win*, 2d ed. (Hanoi: Foreign Languages Publishing House, 1966), p. 100.

2. See John T. McAlister, Jr., and Paul Mus, *The Vietnamese and Their Revolution* (New York: Harper and Row, 1970), pp. 62–69.

3. Saigon *Daily News*, July 5, 1965.

4. *Ibid.*, October 29, 1965.

5. Quoted in Georgie Ann Geyer, "The Illusion Dies," *The Progressive*, February 1969, p. 19.

6. *Quan-Doi Hoc Tap Chinh Tri* (Army Political Studies), Saigon, 1956, p. 20.

7. Quoted in John Sullivan, "Vietnam between Two Truces: Tet and May, 1968," A report for the American Friends Service Committee, May 9, 1968 (mimeographed), p. 27.

8. Quoted in Marjorie Hope, "Guns, Butter—or Chinh Nghia?" *War/Peace Report*, August–September, 1966.

9. See the report on opinion samplings in Vietnam in the Washington *Star*, June 27, 1966.

10. Daniel Ellsberg has perceptively described this and other Vietnamese political attitudes in a "Memorandum for the Record," May 4, 1967.

11. *New York Times*, December 6, 1967.

12. Quoted by Takashi Oka, *Report to the Institute of Current World Affairs*, No. 33 (May 22, 1967).

13. See *Report . . . Regarding Matters in Vietnam . . .* , by Senator Abraham Ribicoff, Permanent Subcommittee on Investigations of the Committee on Government Operations, U.S. Senate, 90th Cong., 2nd Session, May 1968, pp. 18–20; see also "The Women," *Time*, November 8, 1967; for a more recent report, see *Christian Science Monitor*, November 1–3, 1969.

14. *Christian Science Monitor,* May 31, 1967; David Halberstam, "Return to Vietnam," *Harper's,* December 1967.

15. Quoted by Carl D. Robinson, former chief of Research and Programs in Go Cong Province. Interview in Saigon, July 1968.

16. Interviews in Tay Ninh, June 1968.

17. A U.S. government-funded study last year reached this conclusion. See Nathan Leites, "The Viet Cong Style of Politics," RAND Memorandum RM-5487-1-15A/ARPA, May 1969.

18. Quoted by Keyes Beech, Chicago *Daily News,* February 7–8, 1970.

19. Ton That Thien, "Soldiers of Fortune," *Far Eastern Economic Review,* March 14, 1968, p. 443.

20. On South Vietnamese army desertions, see Washington *Post,* June 5, 1968, July 2, 1968, December 12, 1968, July 2, 1969, and Los Angeles *Times,* December 18, 1969.

21. San Francisco *Chronicle,* August 24, 1969.

22. *Christian Science Monitor,* January 5, 1970.

23. San Francisco *Examiner,* December 1, 1968.

24. Translation of original text by Vietnam Education Project, in author's possession.

25. Los Angeles *Times,* June 6, 1969.

26. Washington *Post,* August 30, 1969.

27. Michael Murrow, Dispatch News Service release, April 18, 1969.

28. *Xay Dung* (Saigon), January 21, 1969.

29. Quoted in Peter Schmid, "Free Indochina Fights against Time," *Commentary,* January 1955.

30. *Vietnam News, Views,* August 1968, published by Vietnam Education Project, Washington, D.C.

31. Saigon *Post,* July 16, 1968.

32. Saigon *Daily News,* January 24, 1968.

33. *New York Times,* November 6, 1969.

34. Saigon *Post,* May 15, 1968.

35. Quoted by George McT. Kahin in *The New Republic,* October 14, 1967.

36. *New York Times,* September 28, 1969.

37. *Time,* October 3, 1969, p. 13.

38. *New York Times,* November 26, 1969.

39. *Vietnam: December, 1969,* staff report for the Committee on Foreign Relations, U.S. Senate, February 2, 1970, pp. 12–13.

40. See D. Gareth Porter, "The Diemist Restoration," *Commonweal,* July 11, 1969.

41. See *Christian Science Monitor,* September 26, 1969; Washington *Post,* October 12, 1969; Robert Shaplen, "Letter from Saigon," *New Yorker,* January 31, 1970.

42. *Vietnam: December, 1969,* p. 12.

The Destruction of a Society

by Tran Van Dinh

Our peasants will remember their cratered rice fields and
defoliated forests, devastated by an alien air force that seems
at war with the very land of Vietnam. Villagers will remember their hamlets uprooted from the earth, all to no purpose. And our city dwellers and our intellectuals will mark
how, while saving Vietnam, a half million American soldiers
are suffocating it with their fantastic wealth, their gadg-
etry, their promiscuous virility and their destructive inno-
cence . . .

—Dr. Ton That Thien
Dean of the School of Social Sciences, Van Hanh University, Saigon;
former Press Officer of President Ngo Dinh Diem; former Minister of
Information in the Tran Van Huong Cabinet in 1969

(Statement in the *New York Times,* June 11, 1968)

I see battlefields on which we can destroy anything we locate
through instant communications and the almost instantaneous application of highly lethal power . . . In Vietnam

*Tran Van Dinh served in the South Vietnamese Cabinet in 1960 as
Director General of Information and member of the National
Security Council, and was chargé d'affaires in 1963 in the South
Vietnamese embassy in Washington, D.C. He is the author of* No
Passenger on the River *and co-author of* The Asian Revolution and
Australia. *He is now professor of humanities at Old Westbury Col-
lege of the State University of New York.*

where artillery and tactical air force inflict over two thirds of the casualties, firepower is responsive as never before. It can rain destruction anywhere on the battlefields within minutes, whether friendly troops are present or not . . .

—General William C. Westmoreland
Former commander of the U.S. forces in Vietnam and now Chief of Staff of the U.S. Army
(Speech at the U.S. Army Association, October 14, 1969)

The ruthless and deliberate destruction of the Vietnamese society, a desperate military effort to win a "people's war" with modern conventional weapons, is rooted in the U.S. policy-makers' indifference toward, and ignorance of, the Vietnamese people, their history, their culture and their revolution. As even Henry A. Kissinger, President Nixon's assistant on national security, has said, "It would be difficult to imagine two societies less meant to understand each other than the Vietnamese and the American." [1]

Many Americans are reluctant to recognize that the Asians have a history and civilization and that they value life as much as Westerners. For example, Deputy Defense Secretary David Packard recently repeated the all too familiar cliché that the "Chinese leaders have traditionally placed a rather low value upon human life." [2] An American Indian or a black man in the United States can tell us who has "placed a rather low value upon human life." Nevertheless, that cliché helps Americans to rationalize atrocities committed against Vietnamese villagers, such as the massacre at My Lai and the saturation bombing and artillery fire which destroy Vietnamese villages. [3]

Society, in Vietnamese, is *Xa Hoi,* literally meaning "an association of villages." Hence, the physical destruction of the Vietnamese villages and the "generating" of refugees are tantamount to the destruction of the Vietnamese society itself. The destruction is not only physical; it is spiritual as well. Paul Mus, the late French Orientalist and unrivaled expert on the Vietnamese society, has rightly noted:

> Vietnamese consider the creation of new communities not as political acts but as spiritual ones . . . The ideographical sign XA (village) means "spirit of the earth." It is composed of two characters or roots: *thi* and *tho,* the first meaning everything that refers to spirits and the other expressing the notion of that which is earthly . . . Both characters together give the idea of a gathering place for individuals sacrificing to the spirits; not to the spirits in general but to the patron of the village whose altar is expressed by the character XA in one of its basic meanings. In the consciousness of the Vietnamese masses, the word XA has a central value. It unfolds a landscape, not a physical landscape but a sociological landscape. Yet we have observed that the physical landscape of Vietnam reflects the pattern of the country's society and that within that society the village or XA comes before all else; one belongs to the village before one belongs to oneself . . .[4]

To Vietnamese people, society is made not only of the living but of the dead as well—"more of the dead than the living"[5]—reflecting the deep tradition of ancestor worship. It is therefore impossible for a Vietnamese not to feel an acute pain and a deep anger when he reads this account of the desecration of his dead:

> a hunt for Viet Cong graves . . . took place a few weeks ago in a district not far from Saigon. Convinced that during an artillery and air bombardment of the 6th VC Battalion several guerrillas had been wounded or killed, one battalion of the U.S. 199th Brigade (spearheading Operation Fairfax) made a search of the area the next day and found twenty-nine graves that looked quite fresh. A brigade physician was dispatched to the scene to dig up the graves and examine the bodies. He did so and concluded they were indeed "fresh" enough to permit the brigade to claim twenty-nine killed in action. The statistics of the body count may seem

ghoulish, but they are a vital concern to army officers under the whiplash of superiors demanding "proof" of progress.[6]

In Vietnam, American soldiers leave neither the living nor the dead at peace. Furthermore, the Vietnamese society is made not only of the living and the dead human beings, but of trees, flowers and animals, especially water buffaloes, the eternal and faithful companions of the Vietnamese peasants. With the war, they have all become targets and victims.

While the Vietnamese society is "an association of villages," the village is an association of *ho* (families, or clans). As in China, the Vietnamese society can be termed a system of "familiocracy," where, according to Dr. Y. P. Mei, "An individual is an individual only rarely and by abstraction, as it were." [7]

The cohesion of the Vietnamese society and the stability of the Vietnamese family require its members to respect a number of virtues derived from the harmonious blending of Confucianism, Buddhism and Taoism which form the spiritual foundation of the society. These virtues are: *can* (industry), *kiem* (thrift), *liem* (honesty), *chinh* (straightforwardness). The leaders in North Vietnam preach and live according to these rules. The leaders in the South make reference to them, and then disregard them.

The last thirty years of war and internal conflict have transformed a great part of the Vietnamese society, especially the urban areas in the South, into a community dominated by thieves, dishonest merchants and lazy and corrupted officials. The moral virtues which have constituted the fiber of the Vietnamese society through the ages are disappearing. Since 1965 the massive introduction of American men and money into an already fragile, disrupted society has accelerated the disintegration of the Vietnamese system of values.

A Vietnamese Catholic priest, Father Nguyen Dinh Thi, said on January 22, 1970:

The Americans cannot help the Catholics to keep strong their faith although they may give money to build churches and seminaries. For the nature of the American capitalist and colonialist system is in itself anti-religious. The concrete example is the degradation of morality in South Vietnam since the Americans came . . .

To many Vietnamese the obvious sign of that degradation is the increasing number of prostitutes. Figures on the number of prostitutes are hard to come by, but there are an estimated 100,000 to 300,000 bar girls and prostitutes in Vietnam today.[8] It may be argued that prostitution is a natural companion of any army in any war. However, the prolonged presence of hundreds of thousands of well-paid American troops, who do not make even a minimal effort to understand the Vietnamese society and culture, has caused prostitution to be bitterly resented by the Vietnamese.

The Vietnamese look at prostitution as a degrading profession forced on women who otherwise would be happy as mothers and wives. The nationally known and most admired Vietnamese novel, *Kim Van Kieu,* is about the "pale fate" and the stormy life of Thuy Kieu, a beautiful woman from a middle-class family who had to sell her body to save her father and brother, victims of slanderous accusation by a silk merchant and corrupt government officials. Vietnamese do not hate prostitutes as such, but they do resent and hate the society and the people who force Vietnamese girls to become prostitutes. Today Americans and powerful Vietnamese officials are blamed for the proliferation of "blue castles" (brothels) in South Vietnam.

In a speech on March 7, 1969, in Boston, Ngo Vinh Long, a Vietnamese graduate student in East Asian Studies at Harvard University, said:

A recent Vietnamese study reveals that in the Cap St. Jacques area of South Vietnam, most of the Vietnamese soldiers' wives have become bar girls and prostitutes for the

Americans in order to feed themselves . . . Daily newspapers from Saigon are full of stories about Vietnamese soldiers robbing and committing suicide either because they cannot support their families or because their wives are sleeping with Americans.

In the process of evolution, all human societies develop a hierarchy of values which the masses generally accept. In Vietnam, that hierarchy of values has been and continues to be, in order of importance and respect: *si* (scholars, intellectuals), *nong* (peasants, farmers), *cong* (workers), *thuong* (merchants), *binh* (soldiers). While in North Vietnam, the government is in theory and in practice an alliance of workers, peasants and intellectuals, the regime in South Vietnam is a mafia of soldiers (the last in the Vietnamese hierarchy of values) and rich speculators, such as the notorious pharmacist Nguyen Cao Thang, a close adviser to President Thieu. Worse yet, the generals in South Vietnam are the Vietnamese Benedict Arnolds. Of the fifty-four South Vietnamese generals, fifty-two fought with the French against their own people.[9] Vice President Nguyen Cao Ky himself, in a moment of candor, confessed that "the corruption is among us, among our leaders. Nine out of ten are corrupted."[10] President Nixon's Vietnamization program perpetuates the U.S. support of the alliance between the military and the profiteers who have every interest in continuing the war.

While the generals and war profiteers get wealthier, the war has torn nearly all other Vietnamese families apart— physically, morally and economically. In addition to the death toll and the wanton destruction of homes, war-caused inflation is one of the major reasons for the disruption. The cost of living is galloping at a rate of at least 30 percent yearly. A sergeant in the ARVN with eight years' service makes 5,555 piasters a month (about fifteen U.S. dollars at current black market rates and less than fifty dollars at the official rate of exchange). This is only enough to buy a month's rice supply for a family of five. A policeman makes about 4,500 piasters (eleven dollars) a year.[11] Prices of commodities have skyrocketed since the promulgation of the so-called austerity tax in October 1969, and it is the common people of Vietnam who suffer.

In times of torment, and true to the traditions of the Vietnamese society, the authentic feelings of the people are not deeply and faithfully expressed by government representatives or by newspaper columnists but are revealed by the poets, writers and that mysteriously anonymous voice of the land, the *Ca Dao*.

In an unpublished study, John Balaban, a former member of the International Voluntary Services in South Vietnam, defines the *Ca Dao* as "free songs" which "reflect the deepest components of the Vietnamese soul. It is an oral literature that began several thousand years ago . . . *Ca Dao* are humorous, wistful and sage comments on sex, love, marriage, loneliness, war, religion and social order."

Vietnam is a land of *Ca Dao* and poets. In recent years, the *Ca Dao* have reflected the sad face of the mutilated Vietnamese society:

> *Thi rot tu tai anh di trung si*
> *Em o lai nha lay My nuoi con*
> *Mot mai non nuoc vuon tron*
> *Anh ve thay My con day nha.*

I flunked my baccalaureate examinations and was drafted as a
    corporal in the army.
You, my darling, stay home, sleep with Americans to feed our
    children.
One day when the mountains and the rivers are square and
    round [peace]
I will come home and see the house full of little Americans.

Throughout Vietnamese history, poets have been in the vanguard of protest as they are today. On April 5, 1970, the famed poet-singer, Trinh Cong Son, together with other

artists, writers and poets of the ancient imperial city of
Hue, signed a petition to protest the Saigon government's
suppression of students' rights, the arrests and torture of
students, and the repression of war veterans' demonstrations. The petition also condemned the "United States for
having used Vietnam as a battlefield to test destructive
weapons, to unleash the blind, powerful and inhuman
forces of an imperialist technological, exploiting monster."
Long known as the spokesman against this war "which is
tearing our nation and leading to the extinction of our
race," Son is much admired by the young. The government
has tried hard to silence him, but his songs and poems continue to circulate among the population:

> On a stormy day, I walked alone
> My lips murmur your name
> and the name Vietnam
> Feeling close to you in the language of our race
> I want to love you, love Vietnam.
> Growing up accustomed to sounds of shots
> Explosions of mines
> My hands have no use
> My lips have no use
> I've all but forgotten the language of Man.
>
> (translated by Vo Dinh)

Another poet, Thi Vu, cried in despair:

> If Peace demands such sacrifice
> Then let me die
> And bring light to our future.
>
> (translated by Vo Dinh)

Like any other community of men, the Vietnamese society has its own problems, its deep hopes and its profound
aspirations. A fierce determination to preserve Vietnamese
independence, territorial integrity and unity has united the
Vietnamese people in their common efforts throughout a
long history of both continuity and revolutions. It is a

well-known fact (except to men like former Vice President Hubert Humphrey who once stated that "the new fact in Vietnam is nationalism—there never had been any nationalism in Vietnam" [12]) that the intense Vietnamese nationalism has helped them, a small nation, to defeat the invading armies of great powers (China, Mongolia and France) in the past and to resist the Americans today. To the Vietnamese, independence means simply the absence of foreign troops in their "mountains and rivers."

If the Vietnamese have been successful in defending their country against foreign aggression at the cost of much blood, tears and suffering—a defense made possible by protracted warfare conducted by an army of peasants and intellectuals—they have also learned that territorial and racial unity are harder goals to attain. Nonetheless, there are strong bonds of feeling which unite all Vietnamese. On July 1, 1966, when the U.S. Air Force bombed Hanoi suburbs, the Viet Nam *Guardian* in Saigon editorialized: "The explosion of the bombs in the Hanoi area—which tears the heart of all of us—makes us ask ourselves for whom our compatriots in North Vietnam and a section of our compatriots here in the South have been forced to suffer and die."

The principle of Vietnam's unification and territorial integrity has been affirmed and formalized by the constitutions of the regimes of both the North and the South by the establishment in 1954 of a *temporary* demarcation line at the 17th parallel.[13] As early as 1946, Ho Chi Minh enunciated this principle: "Cochinchina [the lower part of present South Vietnam] is a Vietnamese land. It is the flesh of our flesh, the blood of our blood . . ." In the same year he told the Vietnamese people: "Our compatriots in Nam Bo [Cochinchina] have accepted so much sacrifice in so many months to keep the mountains and the rivers intact for our fatherland. All our compatriots in the whole country are grateful to the compatriots in Nam Bo. Our compatriots in

Nam Bo are citizens of Vietnam. Rivers may dry up, mountains may erode, but this deep truth will remain forever . . ."

Independence and unity for Vietnam would mean very little in the absence of social justice for the people. As in other former colonies, to achieve social justice requires the elimination of the social ills created mainly by feudalism and colonialism. Even President Ngo Dinh Diem acknowledged this concept at the outset of his rule in 1954. The slogans of his regime were: *Bai Phong* (elimination of feudalism), *Diet Thuc* (destruction of colonialism), and *Chong Cong* (opposition to Communism); but they remained only slogans. His regime gradually became autocratic and feudalistic. The increasing number of U.S. advisers in Vietnam revived in the minds of Vietnamese the memory of French colonialism.

Beginning in 1955, Diem embarked upon a ruthless campaign of "Communist denunciation" which degenerated into a repression of all opposition to his rule. Because of the political realities of Vietnam, it remains very difficult, if not impossible, to claim to be antifeudalist and anticolonialist at the same time you are claiming to be anti-Communist. The Vietnamese masses have observed Communist deeds, not only their words, and have concluded that the Communists have been the champions of anticolonialism and antifeudalism since 1930.

Vietnam is an agricultural country. Social ills cannot be eliminated without a radical program of land reform. Successive South Vietnamese governments, with the help of the best experts from the United States, have devised several plans of land distribution,[14] the latest of which was proclaimed by President Thieu not long ago. But these plans are useless pieces of paper for the simple reason that those who are charged with the implementation of the reforms they propose are landowners themselves. A South Vietnamese military commander who comes with his troops

to "pacify" a village is, if not a landowner himself, usually
followed by a returned landowner. This is the fundamental reason why "pacification" under any form and
under any Saigon regime has failed, despite the official
American reports of "progress."

The massive American military and economic aid to a
regime which relies on foreign troops for its survival and
therefore is not independent, which is feudal and not interested in any serious redress of social injustices, contributes
to the destruction of the basic hopes of the people it claims
to save. As Henry Kissinger has noted:

> One ironic aspect of our war in Vietnam is that while we
> profess an idealistic philosophy, our failures have been due
> to our excessive reliance on material factors. The Commun-
> ists, by contrast, holding to a materialistic interpretation,
> owe many of their successes to their ability to supply an
> answer to the question of the nature and foundation of po-
> litical authority.[15]

The destruction of the Vietnamese society by the massive
American intervention in South Vietnam has no precedent
in the history of my country. If the war continues, the dam-
ages may be beyond repair. Being a Vietnamese is more
than merely a nationality. It is also a state of mind and an
act of faith, as affirmed by Ly Thuong Kiet, a Vietnamese
ruler who defeated the invading Sung Chinese in 1077,
when he said that Vietnam is "written down in the Book
of Heaven." Therefore, while bombs are raining down all
over the country, the opposition forces in Saigon and the
leaders of North Vietnam and the NLF pursue their plan
for a Vietnam of the future. Certainly the mission of re-
building Vietnam will not be entrusted to those who are today allied with foreign powers to destroy the land of Vietnam and its independence and unity.

The reconstruction of the Vietnamese society, of the
"association of villages," will have to start at the village

level along "socialist" lines ("socialism" in Vietnamese is *Xa Hoi Chu Nghia,* the doctrine of the association of villages). It can only be accomplished by those persons who are today bolstering Vietnamese optimism, Vietnamese romanticism—in short, the Vietnamese soul. Even the aristocratic former American pro-consul of South Vietnam, Ambassador Henry Cabot Lodge, admitted that "For years, the only people who have been doing anything for the little man, to lift him up, have been the Communists." [16] But the form of government of Vietnam will be left to the Vietnamese to decide without any interference or approval by foreign Communist powers, or by Mr. Lodge.

The most remarkable thing about this cruel war is that neither the Vietnamese in the North nor the people in the South hate the American people. Visitors from the United States to Hanoi can testify to this. Dr. George Roth of San Francisco, a member of the Committee of Responsibility, who returned in late April 1970 from a visit to South Vietnam and has seen the deplorable condition of hospitals there, told Nicholas Von Hoffman of the Washington *Post:* "If the Vietnamese hated us, they'd be exhausted and would have died by now, but they don't hate us; they have an elegant contempt for us. They call us big-nosed and they say, 'One day you will go, and when you go the rain will come and the rain will wash away your every smell . . .' " [17]

Most, if not the overwhelming majority, of the Vietnamese, would agree with the Vietnamese major, a former poet who has become a major in the ARVN, who said to Richard Hammer: "It would be nice if the Americans would go and help defend someone else's freedom for a change." [18]

NOTES

1. Henry A. Kissinger, "The Viet Nam Negotiations," *Foreign Affairs,* January 1969, p. 220.

2. Associated Press release, May 22, 1970.

3. See *One Morning in the War* (New York: Coward-McCann, 1970), by Richard Hammer; and *My Lai 4* (New York: Random House, 1970), by Seymour M. Hersh. See also my reviews of these two books in the *Saturday Review* of May 30, 1970.

4. Paul Mus and John T. McAlister, *The Vietnamese and Their Revolution* (New York: Harper Torchbooks, 1970), p. 4; pp. 117–18. See also Paul Mus, *Vietnam: Sociologie d'une Guerre* (Paris: Editions du Seuil, 1952).

5. *The Vietnamese and Their Revolution*, p. 118.

6. From a column by Rowland Evans and Robert Novak datelined Saigon in Washington *Post* of October 5, 1967.

7. In Charles A. Moore (ed.), *Status of the Individual in East and West* (Honolulu: University of Hawaii Press, 1968), p. 340.

8. Nguyen-Tang Canh and Don Luce, "An Approach to Post-War Service Priorities in South Viet-Nam," October 1969.

9. *I. F. Stone's Weekly*, December 29, 1969.

10. Interview with Oriana Fallaci, Washington *Post*, April 7, 1968.

11. *New York Times*, June 1, 1970.

12. *New York Times*, November 11, 1967.

13. Tran Van Dinh, "Reunification: Key to Peace in Vietnam," *War/Peace Report*, December 1966.

14. Distribution of communal land had been traditionally practiced in Vietnam, but in 1477 King Le Thanh Tong systematized it, and the state set up "state farms" on uncultivated land.

15. Kissinger, *op. cit.*, p. 215.

16. *New York Times*, February 27, 1966.

17. Washington *Post*, May 27, 1970.

18. The final sentence in Hammer's excellent book *One Morning in the War: Tragedy at Son My*.

Vietnam: The Human Costs

by Jerry M. Tinker

THROUGHOUT HISTORY the bystanders—civilians, women and children—have been the victims of the crossfire of war. The image of burning villages and smoldering homes, of refugees fleeing across devastated landscapes, is as old as war itself. That such devastation should occur in Vietnam is, of course, not surprising. What is surprising, almost beyond comprehension, is the *extent* to which it is true of Vietnam.

As every American knows who has watched the war unfold nightly on television, Vietnam has been a peculiarly brutal conflict—brutal not only visually but statistically. More than most wars, Vietnam has caught the civilian bystander in a crossfire that has been both military and political.

As the accumulating facts and reports have revealed the terrible toll in civilian life and property in Vietnam, the confidence and support Americans had for the war at the

Jerry M. Tinker has worked and studied in South and Southeast Asia for more than five years and was a member of a field investigation team (1966–67) sponsored by the Department of Defense to work in South Vietnam. He has written several articles and essays on Vietnam and was editor of Strategies of Revolutionary Warfare. *He is now a Ph.D. candidate at the American University in Washington, D.C.*

outset have slowly eroded. Although President Nixon has talked of a possible future "bloodbath" against South Vietnamese civilians should the United States withdraw, the obvious reality of Vietnam is that the bloodbath started long ago and will continue as long as the war continues. Just how brutal this bloodbath—here and now—has actually been can be seen by reviewing a few statistics. Most attention has been focused on the toll taken of combatants —on the 41,415 American GI's killed and the 272,738 wounded, the 3,761 Allied troops killed, the 105,345 South Vietnamese dead, and the 621,549 Viet-Cong and North Vietnamese killed since the war began.[1]

But an even greater human cost has been borne by the bystanders of this war: the civilian noncombatants. For example, by conservative estimate, over 300,000 South Vietnamese civilians have been killed. Nearly 700,000 have been wounded.[2] And of these one million casualties, a number of medical observers estimate that as many as 60 percent have been under sixteen years of age.[3] The current rate of wounded civilians, according to official admissions to hospitals (and not counting those villagers who never make it to hospitals), is approximately 4,300 per month[4]— although the figure is probably much higher than that.

Over 10,000 war orphans now seek homes in Vietnam, and 82,000 war widows are officially registered, leaving about 200,000 to 250,000 children without fathers.[5] Some 36,000 amputees were awaiting treatment in South Vietnamese hospitals in 1968 alone,[6] and, as the recent veterans' strike in Saigon shows, the ranks of the maimed and disabled grow each month. And on top of it all, a cumulative total of over four million refugees have been dislocated since the war escalated in 1964, with over half a million still officially unresettled and many thousands more "unofficially" languishing in temporary quarters.[7] And the grim statistics go on—all in a nation with a population of less than eighteen million.

Only a few years ago, at the outset of the American involvement in Vietnam, public opinion in this country was greatly exercised over statistics of Viet-Cong terrorism—the assassinations of South Vietnamese civilians and officials. They represented a ruthless toll in human life, and it shocked Americans in 1960, when, in that year alone, 1,400 local Vietnamese civilians were reported killed by Viet-Cong terrorists. But as repugnant as that terrorism was and is, the Viet-Cong, in most instances, sought to be discriminating in their targets, killing key local officials and civilians tied to the government which, in their eyes, was the enemy.

Today, subsequent to the massive American intervention in Vietnam, the United States and its allies are causing—at official, conservative estimates—over 25,000 civilian deaths per year, or fifteen times more than the highest toll of Viet-Cong terrorism. More South Vietnamese civilians are killed now in one month by Allied activity than in a whole year of Viet-Cong terrorism. Tragically, most of today's civilian deaths are simply victims of indiscriminate bombings and random artillery fire.

That the cost in human life and property should be so great in so small an area and in so local a conflict says something both about the unique character of the war in Vietnam and the nature of the American military response to it.

I.

From the ouset, Vietnam has been a war for *people,* not territory. In a guerrilla-type insurgency, the key to "victory" is political allegiance, or at least compliance, and not terrain held. People thus become both the targets and the objective of the conflict. They are the "hearts and minds" to be won, the "water" in which the insurgent "fish" swims, and they are the substance of "pacification," "liberation," "civic action," "agitprop," "revolutionary development," "political reeducation," and all the other slogans, tactics and methods which have proliferated in Vietnam. Such a situation intensifies the involvement of "the people," who, in other kinds of warfare, would be considered "noncombatants" and only inadvertently victimized as military targets. In Vietnam, however, they are at the heart of the conflict.

The introduction of American troops in 1965 exacerbated the problem and made their suffering even more intense. For, in an effort to find a "front line" where it could employ the conventional tactics with which it was familiar, the U.S. military tried to transform the Vietnam guerrilla insurgency into a more manageable and traditional "conventional" war. Only in such a conventional war setting could American generals employ the massive firepower and sophisticated technology at which they excel. However, by this very transformation—involving, as it does, use of a technology which by nature is indiscriminate—the United States for all practical purposes ignored the fact that a guerrilla insurgency is a war fought by and for peasants, in which the use of military force must be politically relevant and highly discriminate. The inevitable result was that the U.S. military's "conventional tactics" destroyed a large portion of the society it set out to save, as well as many of the "hearts and minds" it sought to win.

Much of the human cost of Vietnam has stemmed from the string of ill-considered and maladministered programs of population control and pacification launched by the U.S. and South Vietnamese military since the Viet-Cong insurgency began. Designed to protect South Vietnamese villagers from Viet-Cong harassment and control, these programs all too frequently were as coercive and destructive as the Viet-Cong.

One of the earliest illustrations is the now famous "strategic-hamlet" program, a program that produced the first sizable dislocation of rural Vietnamese and set the pattern for all subsequent population-control plans. Started in early 1962, the "strategic hamlets" were set on the British model in Malaya. Villagers were to be relocated in semi-fortified communities in order to insulate them politically and physically from the insurgents. As an inducement and a political incentive to move, villagers were to be given by the government new social and economic benefits, such as new schools, dispensaries, agricultural aid, etc.

Unfortunately, in Vietnam, the plan never quite worked.[8] Although American advisers were initially most enthusiastic over the program, it began to fail partially because it was a mindless copy of the British experience in Malaya, lifted by Americans, lock, stock, and barrel, for use in Vietnam. But several basic elements that produced success in Malaya were absent in Vietnam. For instance, in Malaya the villages to be resettled were largely temporary, whereas in Vietnam the people to be moved were from long-established hamlets spread over a wide area of rice paddy. In Malaya the British could play upon the ethnic conflict between Malays and Chinese, whereas in Vietnam no such clear antagonism existed between the Viet-Cong and South Vietnamese (often both were from the same hamlet).

The basic reason, however, for the failure in Vietnam was that the resettlement project was approached in a totally coercive and dictatorial manner by the regime of President Ngo Dinh Diem. Indigenous villagers with strong local roots were forced into new hamlets, often built with their forced labor. Frequently they were not compensated with the promised social and economic aid.

After two years, the strategic-hamlet program had become a political as well as strategic disaster. What started as a highly touted plan to attain local village security and, therefore, allegiance ended in bitterness and the dislocation of rural communities. Beyond this, the newly fortified hamlets turned out to be militarily ineffective, for no systematic effort was made to root out the local Viet-Cong cadre. Hence, although the hamlet had a barbed-wire fence, a moat, and a high gate which was locked each night, the local Viet-Cong militia would simply be locked up inside as well. As hamlets were relocated, so, too, were the guerrillas.

The ingredients for failure that doomed the strategic-hamlet program—poorly conceived, coercively implemented, and military in emphasis—have haunted every pacification and population-control program launched since that time. By 1966 the approach to population control (although it was still ostensibly to "protect" villagers from the Viet-Cong) became so crude that it all too often consisted of the worst kind of coercion: the forcible evacuation of villagers by U.S. Army trucks or helicopters to refugee "resettlement" areas.

With the introduction of American combat troops in 1965 the character and priority of pacification and population control changed as well. No longer were relocation programs on as limited a scale as the strategic hamlets. With half a million foreign troops "sweeping and clearing" the countryside, deliberately generating refugees, and bombing free-fire zones, the whole basis of population control changed.

Significantly, the term "the other war" came into existence, and was used by both President Johnson and the military to refer to pacification and population control. That these aspects of the conflict—the political and sociological heart of an insurgent conflict—should suddenly be considered the *other* war, while the U.S. military's conventional activity became *the* war, suggests how thoroughly the character and conduct of the war changed. With that, the end came to low-level counter-insurgency programs of economic aid, military advisers and Special Forces teams, and a largely conventional war began (the

U.S. marines even waded ashore at Danang à la World War II in Iwo Jima style).

The strategic-hamlet program, although a failure, nonetheless set the precedent for further and equally ill-considered programs of population relocation which, when undertaken by large U.S. military units, simply became excuses for the generation of thousands of refugees. A deliberate policy of forcible evacuation of villagers—often on a mass scale—resulted in a massive refugee problem in many areas and created one of the more unfortunate human costs of the war.

II.

Refugee movement in South Vietnam after the Geneva settlement in 1954 began in a small way.* Although some of the movement reflected normal rural-urban demographic shifts, a perceptible refugee movement was reported in the delta province of Long-An where a number of village officials and landlords began to take refuge from Viet Cong actions in 1959.[9] In the central highlands, some 10,000 *montagnards* reportedly had fled from Viet-Cong control by 1962, with one source indicating that perhaps as many as "150,000 mountain tribesmen out of a total of about 700,000 sought refuge in government-controlled areas." [10]

It was not until 1964–65, however, that refugee movement reached major proportions. The heavy spring floods had displaced thousands of families in the central coastal regions. Before these people could be resettled, a major rural-population displacement began, precipitated by the

* Refugee movement immediately after the Geneva Accords consisted of an estimated 900,000 northerners, mostly Catholics, who fled south to escape the new regime of Ho Chi Minh. Refugees since that major movement are more accurately called "displaced persons," for they have moved *within* the borders of South Vietnam, traveling, on the average, only six to twelve miles.

simultaneous Viet-Cong military build-up in central Vietnam and the large-scale introduction of American troops to check the so-called summer offensive of 1965.

Refugee movement since then (when it has not been caused by forced evacuations) has been the result of events tied to both political and military pressures that have varied somewhat from one region to the next. A comprehensive picture of this voluntary refugee movement was first documented in a U.S. government-sponsored survey of refugee problems in 1966–67.[11] This writer, along with a team of two U.S. social scientists and twelve Vietnamese interviewers, studied the growth of the refugee problem in two key provinces: Phu-Yen Province along the central coast, where large Allied units were operating; and Dinh Tuong Province, three hundred miles south in the Mekong Delta, where only South Vietnamese troops were stationed. A large sample of refugee families in the two provinces were interviewed about their reasons for moving from their homes. As the refugees talked, an interesting insight emerged as to their view of the war. Typically, it was complex (as were their reasons for moving), but their responses revealed that after 1965 the average villager found himself thoroughly hammered from both sides.

The lives of many refugees, as we have seen, had first been disrupted in the early 1960's by a combination of Viet-Cong organizing activities and government "protective" responses, such as the strategic-hamlet program. Viet-Cong activities mostly consisted of forced labor, taxation and political coercion. In Phu-Yen Province, for example, 20 percent of the refugees complained of being conscripted to do forced labor—from digging trenches and bunkers, and serving as battlefield coolies, to making sharpened *punji* sticks for booby traps. Another 7 percent complained of heavy taxation of their rice crop and of the perpetual threat of compulsory attendance at "political reeducation" sessions in the remote hills. Another 28 percent spoke of fear of reprisals if they did not cooperate fully with the Viet-Cong. Worst of all, many refugees' source of livelihood had been cut when they could no longer work their fields full time or take their goods to market when the roads were sabotaged by the Viet-Cong.

On top of this disruption, the Allies in 1965 added to the villager's woe by vastly increasing military activity—both ground military operations and, more particularly, artillery fire and aerial bombardment. As conditions grew steadily worse, especially in rural areas, such as Phu-Yen, along the central coast, the first great tide of refugees began to flow. Over 70 percent of the refugees in Phu-Yen and 62 percent in Dinh Tuong moved during this period, depopulating many rural areas.

III.

The view most frequently associated with civilian casualties in Vietnam is of masses of Allied troops sweeping through villages, engaging "the enemy" in ground combat, and killing innocent villagers in the process. Great publicity has been given to the horror of incidences of "atrocities," such as My Lai, which have occasionally occurred during such operations. But the striking fact that emerges from this study of refugee attitudes is that the average Vietnamese villager has been battered and threatened much more by air strikes and artillery than by ground military operations.

Indeed, as refugees list what to them seems most "atrocious"—in Allied bombardment and ground military operations—they more often identify the amount of artillery and bombs that have rained upon them with increasing abundance since 1965. As frightening and as unpardonable as such incidents as My Lai are, and as tragic as some of the side effects of ground operations have been, many Vietnamese refugees feel that the threat from the air holds more terror, and death, than ground operations.

Take, for instance, the interest in refugee reports of indiscriminate killings by Korean troops in Phu-Yen Province in 1966.[12] Without underestimating the horror of those stories, it is significant to note that while 2 percent of the refugees interviewed said Korean actions drove them from their homes or caused them harm, an equal number of those interviewed said Allied artillery killed their relatives and neighbors. In addition, 10 percent more said artillery and bombardment destroyed either their houses or possessions, while another 18 percent expressed generalized fear of artillery as the reason for fleeing their homes.

At the same time, in Dinh Tuong Province over half— 54 percent—of the refugees interviewed said artillery and bombardment were principal reasons behind their decision to move, while only 12 percent said they moved because of ground operations. While 20 percent said their relatives or neighbors were killed or wounded by artillery, only 7 percent were killed or wounded by troop operations.

All this seems to suggest that the Allied "harassment-and-interdiction" artillery fire (called H & I fire) which is intended to stop, or at least harass, Viet-Cong infiltration by randomly hitting presumed supply routes and base areas, has more accurately harassed Vietnamese peasants. Flying over Dinh Tuong today, the land looks as if it had suffered a gigantic case of smallpox. To anyone who has spent a night in a Vietnamese district town and heard the 105-mm howitzers continuously shatter the night's silence, it comes as no surprise that most refugees cite artillery fire as one of the main reasons for fleeing their villages.

Especially unsettling to refugees was the utter randomness of the bombing—the uncertainty as to when or why it would fall. From leftover bombs dumped by pilots into presumed "free-strike zones" to the continuous H & I fire, the devastating fire has hit targets as uncertain and as unseen as the refugees suggest. Considering that the United States has exploded ten times more tonnage of bombs and artillery in Vietnam than it did in all of World War II, it is little wonder that refugees continue to look to the sky with trepidation.

If one criterion for an "atrocity" during ground military operations such as My Lai is a soldier's unwillingness or inability to discriminate between combatant and noncombatant when shooting, then by that same standard it should be incumbent upon the artillerymen to discriminate as much as possible in targeting their fire. Just as My Lai raised questions as to how discriminate American GI's have been, or can be, in shooting "suspected VC," so, too, do the numerous reports of artillery casualties raise questions of how discriminate U.S. and South Vietnamese commanders have been in demarcating "free-fire zones" and in authorizing H & I fire.

While such indiscriminate bombardment may not fall under international law as a "war crime," as My Lai does, and although total casualties may amount to less than the horrors of Hiroshima or Dresden, yet from the standpoint of American "success" in achieving its objectives in Vietnam, this indiscriminate artillery fire has nonetheless been a disaster. South Vietnam is supposed to be a nation being saved from guerrilla insurgency, not an enemy being bombed into submission. The experience of all too many refugees suggests that Vietnam's worst enemy may be its American ally.

This, of course, is the horrible paradox of the Vietnam conflict. For, as in all civil war situations, neither side can actually be fully discriminate. The difference between friend and foe in Vietnam is not externally apparent. Yet the American military persists in waging a conventional war in an unconventional situation where it cannot, and never really could, distinguish the "friendlies," whom it must save, from the "unfriendlies," whom it must fight.

Under such conditions "atrocities," in the sense of grossly indiscriminate acts of destruction, terror and death, are inevitable and will continue.

IV.

Vietnam has become a land of refugees. Their continuing problems and suffering remain a major obstacle to U.S. "success" in Vietnam—even as success is defined by President Nixon. His policy of "Vietnamization," the latest program in "pacification," largely means, under present conditions, the resettlement of refugees. As enunciated by Secretary of Defense Melvin Laird before the U.S. Senate Foreign Relations Committee, Vietnamization means more than just the replacement of U.S. combat troops with Vietnamese forces. It means, he said, "strengthening other institutions outside the military and reforming their practices" and extending pacification.[13] To make progress in pacification, refugees must be resettled.

A flood of statistics has since been released by the administration showing that such progress is being made. President Nixon, in his speech to the nation on April 20, 1970, stated flatly, "We can now say with confidence that pacification is succeeding." Saigon officials assert that this success is due to refugees being resettled at a rapid rate; an overwhelming majority of the population is now under South Vietnamese government control. A school of "new optimists" has emerged in Saigon under the umbrella of Vietnamization.[14]

Upon closer look, however, Vietnamization seems like so many earlier programs: designed more for American domestic consumption than for the realities of Vietnam. Vietnamization is a change of labels rather than a thoroughgoing change of policy. The criteria used in measuring "success" remain as questionable as the statistics upon which they have always been based. For example, under the computerized "Hamlet Evaluation System," it is said that 89.9 percent of South Vietnam's population lives under "government control." [15] Yet, leaving aside the accuracy of the statistic (dubious at best), what exactly does it mean to live under "government control"? To the Nixon administration it is a sign in itself of progress and success in pacification. However, for millions of South Vietnamese refugees, living under "government control" means little more than living in an overcrowded urban area, most likely a slum, existing hand to mouth in a state of poverty. Just fifteen years ago all but 15 percent of South Vietnam's population lived in the countryside. Today, an estimated 60 percent live in urban areas—with Saigon growing from a city of 300,000, for which it was designed, to a sprawling shantytown of three million.[16] These people are all under "government control," but are they "pacified"?

Stated bluntly, the United States and the South Vietnamese government, in order to get people under "government control," have created an urban nation from a rural one, sometimes through deliberate policies of population relocation, sometimes through mindless bombing of rural areas, sometimes through resettlement programs. Either way, it is a rather hollow achievement to count urban slums of discontent as symbols of success in pacification.

Despite optimistic reports of large-scale refugee resettlement under Vietnamization, the refugee problem remains staggering, if for no other reason than in terms of social welfare. Yet, refugee and social-welfare programs still receive low priority compared with military-type programs; in fact, less than one percent of South Vietnam's budget is allocated for refugee aid and resettlement.[17] In many provinces, refugees are ignored by official decree, receiving no aid and no resettlement allowance. Reports show that much of the advertised resettlement of refugees is more a statistical illusion, the result of "bookkeeping" changes ordered by Saigon to improve the image of pacification progress.[18]

In Quang Tin Province, for example, this policy of officially denying the existence of refugees has led first to many refugees being classified as "Viet-Cong suspects" in order that they may receive aid. This occurred in April 1969, when, under Saigon pressure to achieve pacification goals, the senior U.S. province adviser in Quang Tin decided, by fiat, that there were to be more refugees. Existing refugee centers were closed or reclassified as resettlement areas. However, word of this decision never reached the large American field units who continued to produce refugees on "search-and-destroy" and "clear-and-sweep" operations, delivering them by helicopter to province headquarters. But since there was no longer a refugee program, the only way in which aid could be offered these refugees was to classify them as "VC suspects" and then offer them a chance to "defect," whereupon, under the *Chieu Hoi* defection program, they could receive monetary and housing assistance.[19]

Unfortunately this tangled story is not untypical of Vietnam. By every indication, Vietnamization is doing little to alleviate or lessen the continuing human costs of the war. Partly this is because nothing—no program of resettlement or refugee aid—can really lessen the human costs as long as the military conflict continues. To this extent, Vietnamization only disguises this continuing cost by creating the illusion of progress. Yet, today, by official estimate, 4,300 civilians are wounded or killed in Vietnam each month. Military activities which have in the past disrupted and destroyed the political and social fabric of Vietnam continue unabated, even though American participation may have lessened.

The point is that Vietnamization changes nothing. It does not repair the damage or lessen the human costs already incurred, and it does not bring peace by rearranging the actors in war. More important, there is no evidence that Vietnamization can make the South Vietnamese government any more responsive or any more competent than it was when, as a result of its unresponsiveness and incompetence, the United States opted to run South Vietnam's affairs in the first place. The human costs already resulting from that American decision have in themselves destroyed much of the possibility for Vietnamization.

As one American official in Saigon has said: "At best, all Vietnamization does is change the color of the bodies." The bloodbath goes on, and the human costs rise.

NOTES

1. These figures are from official Department of Defense totals and represent cumulative totals up to April 11, 1970. The GI death rate continues at approximately 100 or more per week.

2. These, and the following statistics, were developed by the U.S. Senate Judiciary Subcommittee on Refugees and Escapees, and are based upon five years' investigative study, involving field trips, Senate hearings, and special staff reports. For a complete statement describing the basis for these figures, see the Subcommittee's report recorded in the *Congressional Record*, U.S. Senate, 91st Cong., 1st Session (December 22, 1969), pp. S.17509–S.17510.

3. Hearings, Subcommittee on Refugees and Escapees, U.S. Senate, *Civilian Casualty, Social Welfare and Refugee Problems in South Vietnam*, Part I, U.S. Senate, 91st Cong., 1st Session (Washington, D.C.: Government Printing Office, 1969), p. 124.

4. *Ibid.*, p. 123.

5. Nguyen Tang Canh and Don Luce, "An Approach to Post-War Service Priorities in South Vietnam," unpublished report to the Division of Inter-Church Aid, Refugee and World Service of the World Council of Churches (New York: World Council of Churches, October 1969), p. 14.

6. Subcommittee on Refugees and Escapees, U.S. Senate, *Civilian Casualty and Refugee Problems in South Vietnam, Committee Report on Findings and Recommendations*, U.S. Senate, 90th Cong., 2nd Session (Washington, D.C.: Government Printing Office, 1968), p. 8.

7. Committee on Foreign Relations, U.S. Senate, *Staff Report: Vietnam, December 1969* (Washington, D.C.: Government Printing Office, 1970), p. 4.

8. A great deal has been written on the strategic-hamlet program, but for a good critical assessment see Milton Osborne, *Strategic Hamlets in South Vietnam*, Data Paper 55 (Ithaca, N.Y.: Cornell University Press, 1965); see also Nghiem Dang, *Vietnam: Politics and Public Administration* (Honolulu, Hawaii: East-West Center Press, 1966), pp. 151 ff.

9. Gerald Hickey, *Village in Vietnam* (New Haven, Conn.: Yale University Press, 1964), p. 11.

10. Bernard Fall, *The Two Viet-Nams* (New York: Praeger, 1964), p. 366; also Jerry Rose, "I'm Hit!" *Saturday Evening Post* (March 23, 1963), pp. 35–46.

11. The complete findings and methodology of the survey are reported in *The Refugee Situation in Phu-Yen Province*, by A. Terry Rambo, Jerry M. Tinker, and John D. LeNoir, and in *The Refugee Situation in Dinh Tuong Province*, by Jerry M. Tinker (McLean, Va.: Human Sciences Research, Inc., 1967). Some conclusions of these reports also appeared in "Bombs Redefine War's Atrocity," by Jerry M. Tinker, the Washington *Post* (Washington, D.C., February 15, 1970), p. C-1.

12. "Korean Atrocities Reported in Vietnam," *New York Times* (New York, January 10, 1970), p. 1.

13. Hearings, Committee on Foreign Relations, U.S. Senate, *Briefing on Vietnam*, November 18–19, 1969, U.S. Senate, 91st Cong., 1st Session (Washington, D.C.: Government Printing Office, 1969), pp. 58 ff.

14. Robert Kaiser, "The New Optimists," the Washington *Post* (Washington, D.C., October 29–November 3, 1969).

15. "U.S. Now Assesses Pacification Effort through Computer," *New York Times* (New York, March 3, 1970).

16. Terence Smith, "Refugees Pose Urban Crisis in Saigon," *New York Times* (New York, February 16, 1970), p. 1.

17. Elizabeth Pond, "South Vietnam's Refugees: Aid 'too little, too late?'" *Christian Science Monitor* (Boston, June 4, 1969), p. 1.

18. David Hoffman, "Statistics are Hiding Refugees," the Washington *Post* (Washington, D.C., December 14, 1969).

19. Report to the Subcommittee on Refugees and Escapees, U.S. Senate, Washington, D.C., April 1, 1970. For an example of how refugees are generated and treated, see the excellent study by Jonathan Schell, *The Village of Ben Suc* (New York: Knopf, 1967).

Ecocide in Vietnam

by J. B. Neilands

THE ENVIRONMENT of Vietnam, particularly in the South, has been ravaged by years of war. Added to the widespread destruction caused by modern weapons for the first time in the annals of war, there has been in Vietnam a massive deployment of chemical agents for the systematic destruction of plant life. This has had grave ecological consequences, and has damaged the economy, health and welfare of the civilian population.

Recently a proposal was made by Arthur Galston, professor of biology at Yale University, calling for a new international agreement to ban "ecocide"—the willful destruction of the environment. Such an agreement has a particular urgency for South Vietnam since that country is the scene of a vast American defoliation project involving millions of acres and thousands of square miles. The largest

J. B. Neilands is professor of biochemistry at the University of California at Berkeley. He is the author of more than a hundred research papers on enzymology, iron metabolism and bioinorganic chemistry, and the co-author of Outlines of Enzyme Chemistry. *He was chairman of the Scientists' Committee on Chemical and Biological Warfare and a member of the International Commission of Enquiry into U.S. War Crimes in Vietnam. He traveled to North Vietnam in 1967 at his own expense as an investigator for the Bertrand Russell War Crimes Tribunal.*

part of that project is known as Operation Ranch Hand, a
program of the U.S. Air Force for spraying chemicals on
targets selected by the Army.

This operation has continued in Vietnam, unaffected by
President Nixon's declaration in November 1969 that the
United States would completely renounce the use of biological weapons as well as the first use of lethal or inca-
pacitating chemical weapons. The U.S. military has all
along maintained that its use of herbicides—chemicals designed to kill plants—does not constitute chemical warfare
and, in any case, that the United States is not a party to
any international agreement which outlaws the use of
chemicals in war.

The latter argument is perhaps technically correct in
that the United States, although it initiated the 1925 Geneva Protocol which prohibits the military use of chemical
and biological weapons, never ratified this instrument. On
November 25, 1969, one day after the appointment of
Lieutenant General William R. Peers to investigate the
massacres at My Lai, President Nixon announced his in-
tention to scrap biological weapons and resubmit the Geneva Protocol to the Senate for ratification. Within weeks
after the President's declaration, the Swedish delegation in
the United Nations moved a resolution which specified
that all chemical agents, including tear gas and herbicides,
be covered by the Geneva Protocol. The resolution was approved by a vote of eighty to three; the United States, together with Portugal and Australia, voted against the resolution.

While world opinion clearly argues against herbicides,
the American public seems to be relatively unaware of the
extent to which ecocide is a reality in Vietnam. Confusion
also exists about the methods by which herbicides are used
in that country. This essay is an attempt to clarify both of
these issues.

The U.S. began Operation Ranch Hand on a modest

scale in 1962 and escalated it rapidly until a peak was reached in 1967, when an area of 1.7 million acres were sprayed. Among the current euphemisms about Ranch Hand is that it is simple "defoliation," akin to killing weeds in normal agricultural practice. In fact, the chemicals employed are herbicides, and some of them have been ruled too toxic or too persistent for similar use in U.S. domestic agriculture. A second point to be made about Ranch Hand is that it is also a food-destruction program. For example, in 1965 over 40 percent of the total area sprayed was crop land.

Three major herbicides—designated as agents Orange, Blue, and White from the stripes painted on the drums in which they are stored—were used in Operation Ranch Hand until April of this year. Agent Orange was a favorite herbicide in the military's defoliation program; in 1967 and 1968, the Department of Defense commandeered the entire domestic production of 2,4,5-T (Agent Orange), an amount estimated from U.S. Tariff Commission Reports as about 13 million pounds. In 1969, 3.3 million gallons of Orange were used by Operation Ranch Hand. Then, on April 15, 1970, the Pentagon announced the suspension of 2,4,5-T for use in Vietnam.

The question remains as to why the administration delayed so long in announcing the ban of a chemical whose bad record had been known for many months. Agent Orange, a mixture of 2,4-D and 2,4,5-T, has been the subject of intense discussion since the summer of 1969 when several Saigon newspapers published photos of horribly deformed babies born in villages in heavily defoliated zones. Some of the accounts specifically linked the birth defects to the American defoliation program, and some of the papers which published the reports were closed down by the government of South Vietnam. Subsequently it turned out that in 1966 the National Cancer Institute had commissioned the Bionetics Research Laboratories, Inc., of

Bethesda, Maryland, to study the carcinogenic, mutagenic and teratogenic properties of a number of pesticides and industrial chemicals, including 2,4-D and 2,4,5-T. When information on the extreme teratogenic (thalidomide-like) effects of 2,4,5-T leaked to the public last year, President Nixon's adviser on science and technology, Lee DuBridge, abruptly announced, on October 29, 1969, that this herbicide would be restricted for domestic use starting in January 1970. Congressman Richard D. McCarthy urged President Nixon to ban both the military and domestic uses of 2,4,5-T, but the Washington *Post* on October 31, 1969, reported the Pentagon as saying that the substance would continue to be used in Vietnam.

The powerful American herbicide industry, although painfully aware from their own experience of the toxic properties of 2,4,5-T preparations, was apparently taken entirely by surprise by DuBridge's announcement. There is evidence that the industry took steps to have the order from the White House canceled. The January deadline came and went, and the use of 2,4,5-T continued unabated. Various Federal agencies, such as the Food and Drug Administration and the U.S. Department of Agriculture, moved slowly to eliminate 2,4,5-T. These agencies claimed that the sample tested by Bionetics Laboratories contained 27 parts per million of dioxin, a contaminant formed in the preparation process, and that it may have been the dioxin which gave the 100 percent incidence of birth defects seen in the laboratory animals. According to the U.S. Department of Agriculture, preliminary tests with 2,4,5-T containing one part per million dioxin showed no teratogenic effects, and the Department of Health, Education and Welfare concurred that "the public interest would best be served by waiting for additional research data." A large defoliation project, also involving 2,4,5-T, had previously been initiated by the Forest Service near Globe, Arizona. It caused a great deal of distress to the local inhabitants, who ascribed public health problems and ecological damage to the project.

The debate over the source of the toxicity in preparations of 2,4,5-T was partially resolved in April 1970, when it was revealed that the herbicide itself, as well as the contaminating dioxins, may produce abnormal developments in unborn animals. In a joint announcement, three departments—Interior, Agriculture and Health, Education and Welfare—ordered an immediate halt to interstate sales and shipment of liquid forms of 2,4,5-T and banned all application of the herbicide to food crops. On the same date, April 15, the Pentagon suspended use of 2,4,5-T in Vietnam.

The Dow Chemical Company is the largest manufacturer of 2,4,5-T, and although the quality of their product, as sprayed in both Vietnam and the U.S., is not precisely known, it is estimated to be not more than 90 percent pure. Here are the cautionary notices on Dow's commercial packages of 2,4,5-T:

> May cause skin irritation—avoid contact with eyes, skin and clothing—keep out of reach of children—do not contaminate irrigation ditches or water used for domestic purposes—seller makes no warranty of any kind, express or implied, concerning the use of this product—buyer assumes all risk of use or handling, whether in accordance with directions or not.

As early as 1959 the *Journal of the American Medical Association* carried a description of peripheral neuropathy attributed to 2,4-D, and it was concluded that the herbicide should be "used with caution." Clearly, the toxic properties of 2,4-D and 2,4,5-T have been seriously underestimated, at least for the commercial preparations of the herbicides, although at this time the known toxicity cannot be assigned to a specific chemical ingredient.[2]

Agent Orange was used in Vietnam at thirteen times the recommended concentration for application in the

United States, and it has been estimated that a pregnant
Vietnamese woman drinking less than two quarts of con-
taminated water daily could ingest a quantity of 2,4,5-T
equivalent to a teratogenic dose in laboratory animals.
Dr. Nguyen Son Cao, a physician who has practiced for
twenty-one years in the province capital of Bien Hoa, the
"defoliation capital of the civilized world," claims that the
abortion rate in his patients has doubled in recent years,
apparently as the result of herbicides sprayed on the area.

Since Orange alone accounted for about half of the total
herbicide volume sprayed on Vietnam, a substantial portion of the expected ecological damage can be assigned to
this chemical. Up to one hundred thousand acres of man-
groves have been sprayed, and at the sites where the first
applications were made nine years ago, there is today not
a significant degree of regeneration. The mangrove swamps
furnish an ecological niche for completion of the life
cycles of certain shellfish and migratory fish which provide
an important source of protein in the diet of the population. Experts believe that these delicately balanced associations of plant and animal life may require decades for
restoration.

Although a ban on Orange has been announced, agents
White and Blue are still approved for use in Vietnam.
Agent White is sold under the trade name "Tordon," and
is also a product of the Dow Chemical Company. It is a
fantastically persistent herbicide—comparable to DDT in
its durability—and for this reason it has not been author-
ized for application to a single American crop. In one field
test carried out by Dow and reported in their publication
Down to Earth, less than three and a half percent of the
applied dose disappeared from the soil over a period of
467 days. Agent Orange must be dissolved in an organic
carrier which is susceptible to drift at the tropical tem-
peratures prevailing in Vietnam (accidents in Operation
Ranch Hand have defoliated gardens and crops being cul-

tivated by "friendlies" and even the agricultural plots of the Agricultural College of the University of Saigon). Agent White is water-soluble, and can be dissolved in an aqueous carrier which gives less trouble with drift. Consequently White is used for precision defoliation around airports and populated areas.

The third herbicidal preparation, Agent Blue, is an organic arsenical. It is uniquely capable of killing thin-leaved plants, such as rice, and is used for this purpose in Vietnam. Since the active ingredient in Agent Blue is cacodylic acid, a substance which contains 54.29 percent arsenic, the American Association for the Advancement of Science has asked repeatedly that its use in Vietnam be discontinued. There is no good scientific information available on what happens to cacodylic acid in the soil, but biochemical mechanisms in soil-dwelling microorganisms are capable of returning the substance to an inorganic state, thus rendering it a deadly poison.

The use of starvation as a weapon has been employed many times throughout the history of organized warfare but without very great success. Military forces, in this case the National Liberation Front, can generally forage for themselves. Consequently it is only the weakest segments of the civilian population—children under five, pregnant and lactating women, the aged and the infirm—who are especially victimized by the food-destruction program.

South Vietnam may be subdivided into the large delta of the Mekong—which comprises one third of the total land area—the narrow coastal plains, and the extensive interior highlands. The dominant natural-vegetation types are the broadleaf-evergreen forest, mountain forest, monsoon forest and mangrove associations. A substantial portion of the terrain, particularly in the Mekong Delta, is devoted to rice culture.

South Vietnam had, in fact, one of the best natural en-

dowments for agriculture in Southeast Asia, and, in normal
times, was capable of providing a reasonably adequate diet
of rice and fish for the people of the region. In 1964 South
Vietnam produced over five million metric tons of rice.
Now, however, rice is one of the major imported commodities.

As much as 50 percent of the soil of Vietnam has a high
content of oxides of iron and hydroxide of aluminum. It
must of necessity contain a quantity of organic matter,
furnished by plant growth, to prevent its solidification into
a rocklike formation. Since two applications of herbicides
will kill virtually all of the forest trees, there is a distinct
possibility that some of this permanently denuded land-
scape will be irreversibly lost for future agricultural production.

From 1962 through June 30, 1969 (the only period for
which figures are available), over five million acres in
South Vietnam were sprayed—an area approximately the
size of Massachusetts. The operation is purely American,
although a fiction is maintained that it is somehow under
the control of the government of South Vietnam. The
Saigon government is, in fact, very touchy about the program and considers it to be classified. A former minister of
agriculture, Don That Trinh, accused the Defense Min-
istry of concealing the defoliation program. Responsible
South Vietnamese scientists and officials say they know
nothing about the project, and the Rubber Research Institute in Saigon has been unable to determine the nature
of the chemicals sprayed on their plantations.

Deployment is done with C-123 aircraft fitted with
thousand-gallon tanks, helicopters and ground-spray equip-
ment. On a number of occasions, malfunctioning spray
nozzles in the C-123's have necessitated dumping the entire cargo of chemicals in a half minute instead of the usual
four and one-half minutes. Engine troubles have also
caused the load to be jettisoned. Tan Hiep and Bien Hoa

have in this way been doused with Agent Orange. Although the exposed people complained of various maladies, they received no medical attention after these or any of the other eight similar emergency dumpings which have been reported since 1968.

According to a report in the *New York Times* on June 23, 1970, the C-123 planes which have conducted the spraying in Vietnam were diverted by the invasion of Cambodia into hauling out captured arms and ammunition. This led to a temporary suspension of the defoliation operation during May and June 1970.

Defoliation has not been restricted to South Vietnam, but has also been inflicted on parts of Laos, Cambodia and Thailand. Cambodia, in fact, filed a 9-million-dollar damage claim against the United States for "accidental" defoliation to its eastern province of Kompong Cham in April and May 1969. A total of 173,000 acres were sprayed, including 38,300 acres of rubber plantations, with what appears to have been Agent Orange. International teams of experts have since increased the early estimates of damage, and as a consequence, Cambodian authorities raised the claim to $12.2 million. A final assessment was to have been made in the summer of 1970. (The United States has, in the past, compensated French owners at the rate of $87 per rubber tree defoliated.) The thirty thousand Cambodians living in the defoliated sector—most of them subsistence farmers—saw their crops of fruits and vegetables wither before their eyes.

All animal life on this globe, including man, depends for its existence on plant life, since the latter alone can trap and store, in chemical form, the radiant energy of the sun. Vegetation, however, is by no means the only component of the ecosystem to suffer from defoliation. Destruction of the basic source of nutrition means that all food chains depending on that source are likewise destroyed. Thousands of species of insects, birds and mammals are supported by forest vegetation and contribute, in turn, to the stability of the system.

South Vietnam long has been the habitat of many unique species of animal life, whose existence is now threatened, by the war in general and defoliation in particular. Both the douc langur (monkey) and the Indochinese gibbon, which have been on the verge of extinction for many years, may be wiped out since they feed exclusively on certain plants growing in the heavily defoliated areas. Indochina has also been the home of the world's rarest and most primitive bovines, such as the kouprey, banteng and gaur; one subspecies of these has been reduced to about three hundred head. The rhinoceros is no longer seen in South Vietnam and a number of animal species, including muntjacs (deer) and wild boars, have migrated westward into Cambodia. The status of the elephant is especially delicate, since these magnificent beasts are used as pack animals in the countryside and hence are considered to be "targets of opportunity" for our fighter pilots.

Birds are often sensitive indicators of the quality of the environment, and it is significant that zoologists who have recently visited South Vietnam report sighting no insectivorous or frugivorous species with the exception of barn swallows, which they took to be visitors from the North.

The environmental tragedy attributable to Ranch Hand is enlarged by the incessant bombing. Large sections of the countryside in South Vietnam have taken on the appearance of a moonscape; an estimated 2.6 million bomb craters were created in one year, 1968, from B-52 bomber strikes. These craters provide ideal breeding ponds for mosquitoes.

As well as being terrible in and of itself, the American defoliation operation in Vietnam falls afoul of international law. The United States is party to the Hague Convention of 1907, which limits the destruction of food supplies to those which are used solely by enemy military forces. The Pentagon has yet to prove that the rice fields sprayed with Agent Blue are cultivated exclusively for the National Liberation Front.

World opinion against herbicides was manifested in the United Nations resolution mentioned earlier. Hopefully the UN will be able to create both the legal definition of the term "ecocide" and the means for indictment of those nations which commit this high crime against the environment. In the meantime, ecocide is a fact in South Vietnam.

SOURCES

Army, U.S. Department of the, *Training Circular* 3–16, 1969.

Blumenthal, Ralph, *New York Times,* March 15, 1970.

Galston, A. W., "Military Uses of Herbicides in Vietnam," *New Scientist,* June 13, 1968.

House, W. B., et al., Midwest Research Institute, report, 1967.

Huddle, F. B., "A Technology Assessment of the Vietnam Defoliant Matter," report to the House Committee on Science and Astronautics, 91st Congress, 1969.

Mayer, Jean, "Crop Destruction in Vietnam," *Science,* April 15, 1966.

McCarthy, R. D., *The Ultimate Folly* (New York: Vintage Books, 1969).

Neilands, J. B., "Vietnam: Progress of the Chemical War," *Asian Survey,* March 1970.

Orians, G. and E. W. Pfeiffer, interview in *Scientific Research,* June 9 and 23, 1969; *Science,* May 1, 1970.

Pfeiffer, E. W., "Ecological Effects of the Vietnam War," *Science Journal,* February 1969.

Tschirley, F., "Defoliation in Vietnam," *Science,* February 24, 1969.

Westing, A. H., et al., "Defoliation Damage in Cambodia," *Congressional Record,* 1970, p. 116.

Whiteside, T., "Defoliation," *New Yorker,* February 7, 1970.

Zablocki, C., *Hearings,* Subcommittee on National Security Policy and Scientific Developments, House Committee on Foreign Affairs, November–December, 1969.

The End of American Innocence

by Edmund Stillman

He who would play the angel ends by playing the beast.
—Blaise Pascal

THAT THE WAR in Vietnam has proved a costly adventure
for the United States is possibly the least controversial assertion that could be made about the undertaking, uniting
both the critics of the war and the apologists. There are
now over fifty thousand American dead of all causes and
nearly six times as many wounded. The national losses
have never been reported with real candor, but in the four
and a half years since the Johnson administration's remarkably unprescient decision to intervene in force—in order
to shore up a rapidly disintegrating Saigon government
and hopefully to bring the operation to a rapid close—the
war has swallowed up what may be estimated at over $200
billion and subjected the American economy to strains un-
precedented in severity since the demobilization at the
close of World War II. These costs, in blood and money,
now give every sign of ballooning as the war, once limited
to South Vietnam, is carried to neighboring Laos and

*Edmund Stillman is adjunct professor of international politics
at the School of Advanced International Studies of the Johns Hopkins University, and co-author (with William Pfaff) of* The New
Politics, The Politics of Hysteria, *and* Power and Impotence: The
Failure of America's Foreign Policy.

Cambodia, and indeed, before it is all over, give signs
that it could (in essence, by a reverse domino effect) spread
to Thailand as well.

To prophesy in such dark terms is not to invoke the
apocalypse. It is a sober probability reckoning. The American involvement began in Vietnam in 1954, almost before
the ink on the Geneva Accords was dry. The objective
record of events since that time shows that the war has
inexorably widened—whatever the intentions of the plan-
ners—in geographical scope and in intensity of violence.
The "crisis managers" and "escalation managers" of the
Kennedy and Johnson and now the Nixon years may have
thought they were practicing the art of limited war; but
they seem, all of them, to have forgotten that wars are limited not merely by technique but by a severe restriction of
the ends in view. You cannot fight a limited war for ultimate victory. You can only fight such a war for compromise—and this is precisely what three successive administrations since 1960 have refused to do. Obfuscations about
"winning the peace" rather than "winning the war" do
nothing to mask the reality: the United States has stead-
fastly refused to bargain about the composition of the governing power in Saigon, which is, of course, what the war
was all about from the beginning. Indeed, at this late date,
now that it has put itself in thrall to the Thieu regime
and given endless hostages to fortune, it is not certain that
the Nixon administration, any more than its predecessors,
could bargain even if it so wished.

From the point of view of the professional practice of
diplomacy, this is one of the most appalling features of
the war. The United States has consistently foreclosed
those options which promised a way out of Vietnam by
way of cutting losses. Given the choice between a prudent
hedging of bets and the bold and splashy option which re-
doubled the potential costs as against only problematical

gain, there has been a depressing Pavlovian consistency about the American choice: *toujours l'audace*.

This insouciant American penchant for risk would seem to be the legacy of an impossibly lucky and tragedy-free past—for the characteristic American reaction to dilemma, both on the part of the nation's leaders and the silent majority (which may in fact exist and which may in fact trustingly follow), is to assert and reassert American omnipotence, whatever the contrary evidence provided by the disheartening war itself. Americans are not used to failure. But as Washington stumbles ever deeper into the Southeast Asian bog, the penalties for an all-too-likely future failure also grow. When America finally comes to the end of its Southeast Asian adventure, that end is likely to be bitter indeed. And not the least among the victims of that failure will be American optimism and self-confidence.

This in itself may be no bad thing, since it can be argued that a near-megalomaniac optimism led straight to the American involvement in Vietnam and the consequent compounding of the tragedy in which the Vietnamese people found themselves caught.

Indeed, the illusion of omnipotence underlies the whole quality of overextension which characterizes American policy in Asia, in Latin America and in Europe. But no one who has pondered the American national character and its taste for violence can look forward without foreboding to a day when Americans will find themselves balked at last by history and yet possessing vast power—not merely economic and conventional military power, but nuclear weaponry as well.

For the shorter run, the consequences of the American adventure have already proved dire. It has been the fashion in this country to agonize over the prevalence of anti-Americanism in the world. But the antipathy to America and Americans—often enough merely the spiteful deference weakness and defeat pay to affluence and power—has

existed alongside a genuine long-standing admiration. Not
only Americans have always thought of themselves as a
new dispensation—self-consciously established in the New
World as God's American Israel. Curiously, for all its envy,
the world had always tended to accept Americans at their
own evaluation. *"Amerika,"* Goethe put it, *"du hast's
besser,"* and as early as the opening years of the American
Revolution, the French statesman Turgot had observed:
"All right-thinking men must pray that this people may
arrive at all the prosperity of which they are capable. They
are the hope of the human race . . . They must prove to
the world, as a fact, that men can be both free and peaceful."

For nearly two centuries America functioned as a datum,
a bench mark, for the world—not only as America was,
but as it hoped to be. The American claim to be a chosen
people won more than a passing acceptance, even if sometimes the uneasy acceptance, of the world. Hostile visitors,
such as Charles Dickens and Frances Trollope, to the
America of earlier years betrayed by their very stridency
their grudging half-acceptance of the myth. If Woodrow
Wilson as the self-proclaimed incarnation of international
morality irritated Lloyd George and Clemenceau at Ver-
sailles, their respective peoples certainly displayed no such
reserve when they greeted the American President (and
through him, his nation) when he arrived in London and
Paris. Even the post-World War II intellectual merchants
of St. Germain—like Sartre and Simone de Beauvoir—
who were so savage in their strictures, often seemed, by
the passionate and frequently anti-rational quality of their
anti-Americanism, more like disappointed lovers than anything else.

All this, one fears, is sadly changed in today's world.
Vietnam has put an end to it. During the Korean War,
there were not many who truly believed that American
troops employed germ warfare or massacred civilians as

Pyongyang, Peking and Moscow incessantly proclaimed.
The world did not believe, for the simple reason that, in
those years, it was implausible that the charges were true.
But indiscriminate defoliation, casual "harassment and
interdiction," free-fire zones, search-and-destroy missions
that do not bother to discriminate between neutral and
foe, the all-too-well-attested suspicion that something massive and dreadful did in fact occur at My Lai, and the
not-yet-proven but hardly irrational suspicion that other
My Lai's may have happened—for the world, these actions
have left precious little belief that America is indeed a new
dispensation, in Lincoln's by now banal but ultimately
moving words, "the last, best hope of earth."

Nor, in purely practical terms, is America able to act
effectively—far less, to take the leadership—to damp down
the Middle East crisis or influence East-West negotiations
in Europe while its attention is distracted by remote Southeast Asia and its forces are tied down there.

Saddest of all, after Vietnam it seems that Americans
themselves, let alone our disconsolate European allies,
can no longer believe that America represents a special
dispensation. Nothing could be sadder than the massive
indifference that characterized the American reaction to
the news of My Lai: War was war and "all people" fought
that way. Having deafened the world with their boasts of
cleanliness and virtue for nearly two centuries, the result
of Vietnam is that Americans now shamefacedly excuse
themselves as "no worse" than others. One seems to hear,
from afar, a cold celestial laughter.

It has been asserted that the war in Vietnam represents
a tragic misdirection of funds, and that the war is somehow directly responsible for the alienation of the young
in America, the anger of blacks, the decline of public law-
fulness. Here I confess a certain skepticism. That there is
a connection, some connection, between the war and

these negative phenomena seems self-evident; but a direct connection is harder to prove.

As for the allocation of national resources, moral and intellectual as well as fiscal, the situation is not, as the defense pundits like to say, "a zero-sum game." One doubts that money saved from Vietnam would be expended in significant measure on rehabilitation of the inner city, Head Start programs for blacks and Indians, or anti-pollution. War, as William James recognized long ago, is a heady business, and it is somehow easier to find appropriations for the military than for social regeneration.

On the fiscal level the real damage done is simply that Vietnam is straining the American economy; it is bad for business—not good, as a naïve and fundamentalist Marxist might suggest. On this score one may cite the poor opinion held of the war by the *Wall Street Journal* and the chairman of the board of the Bank of America in his testimony before the Senate in April 1970. (Only a paranoid could see in the editorial board of the *Journal* and in Louis Lundborg leftist minions at work.) If further evidence of the war's pernicious economic effect is needed, the Dow-Jones recent erratic behavior will provide the bad news.

The war's connection with domestic civil disorder, both racial and political, seems to me to be fourfold.

First, while it cannot be denied that the first symptoms of racial militancy predate the massive American involvement in the Vietnam struggle, and while it cannot be denied that campus and other radical political protest has origins in the exhaustion of the nineteenth-century liberal tradition and the contemporary anti-Enlightenment, anti-positivist vogue for politics-by-action rather than politics-by-reflection, nevertheless I do not see how we can deny that the spectacle of gratuitous violence

inflicted on a luckless people engenders a like climate
of violence at home. The spectacle of war is always unsettling (and in the conditions of contemporary, nearly
instantaneous television and motion-picture communication, the spectacle is virtually firsthand), but the spectacle
of seemingly pointless killing and destruction is far more
so. For the intellectual community and the sensitive young
in the United States—whatever the silent majority may
think, assuming that such people really think at all rather
than blindly trust men who in fact have contempt for
them and habitually deceive them—the purposes and
justness of the Vietnam war have never been adequately
demonstrated. (And, lest I be misunderstood, this is because, I think, those purposes and justness cannot be.)

It is possible that the intellectual and the sensitive
among our people might suppress their revulsion against
mass killing in the interests of a demonstrable higher
good—say, the suppression of Hitlerism, or, for that
matter, of a rampant Stalinism. But compunctions cannot
be put to rest when the threat to world peace and a long-
since-outmoded American conception of world order is a
small Asian nation—North Vietnam—which, whatever
the complex legalities of the Vietnam war, seems to be
able to elicit a good deal of selfless support from the native
populations involved. For many people, there has always
been the nagging suspicion that in Vietnam it is the
United States which has somehow, perhaps without con-
scious design, cast itself in the role of aggressor.

Second, there is the melancholy fact that the American
government, which proclaims itself the embodiment of
social order and the principled rule of law, has brazenly
deceived its citizens through three successive administrations, Democratic and Republican. The habitual lack of
candor displayed by the representatives of the Kennedy,
Johnson and Nixon administrations in camouflaging the

steady escalation of the American involvement in the Vietnamese (and now the wider Indochinese) war scarcely offered a steadying example of respect for the inherited constitutional order. Nor, to say the least, do demonstrations that constitutional means of protest are impotent, or that those who usually peacefully protest can be cut down by trigger-happy minions of law and order, establish a climate of reasoned good sense.

Indeed, this squandering of the respect in which the government of the United States has been habitually held by its own citizens—along with the squandering of the popular habit of belief in the government's decisions— may prove in the end the worst cost of the war, to Americans at least.

Third, there seems to me an inescapable fact that the disaffected white middle-class young and the militant blacks of America have quite literally been exposed to ideological infection in Vietnam. It was with some reason that the French and British governments after 1918 hesitated to commit large-scale forces to intervene in the Russian civil war, for to do so was to expose these troops to the blandishments of enemy proletarian propaganda. I do not suppose there are more than a few white American troops in Vietnam who have been enchanted by Viet-Cong ideological pronouncements; one suspects that a somewhat larger number of already disaffected or ambivalent black troops may have been. What has occurred is that the publicity surrounding this combat, and the oft-repeated American determination to make Vietnam a proving ground for a quasi-theological confrontation with "people's wars," have widened the ideological effects far beyond the troops directly engaged. The American government's ideological stance has powerfully contributed to an exaggerated mystique of "national liberation struggles." For the black militants of America, the spec-

tacle of the seemingly invincible United States held in
check by a ragtag Asia irregular army must be an
exhilarating model.

This brings me to my fourth point—namely, that by
presenting a spectacle of public ineptitude in Vietnam, the
leaders of this country (call them the ruling class, the
Establishment, the Military-Industrial-Bureaucratic Complex, or what you will) have revealed themselves as painfully vulnerable to challenge and, conceivably, to defeat.

It should be self-evident that successful authority, governmental or private, rests not on the element of cum-
pulsion but on the willing acquiescence of the rank and
file to the instructions of leaders—in other words, as the
public philosophers have long held, political and social
authority rests ultimately on an element of consent. It is
possible to police an aberrant or defiant one or two percent of the population; it is not possible to do so with the
dissent of even a sizable minority without recourse to an
ever-increasing degree of repression and force. And a
leadership which reveals itself as devoid of inherent authority (and such inherent authority must always rest on
the charismatic qualities of a ruling class, its perceived
competence) is in trouble indeed. Especially is it in trouble
when those in the forefront of protest are those who in
other times most readily, as they did in World War II,
would have sprung to the defense of the country and, in
after years, would be expected to provide the leadership
cadres, the new recruits to the Establishment itself.

One of the great social costs of Vietnam is that the
American political and military leadership has revealed
itself as naked: in effect, the emperor has no clothes. The
consequent domestic revolt of those who for so long held
their hostilities in abeyance, or, in the case of the blacks,
simply repressed them out of fear and awe of the white
governing authority, should come as a surprise to no one.

·   ·   ·

There are other social costs to the war in Vietnam. Implausible as it may seem to those who are likely to deplore the American involvement there, not the least of these costs has been the destruction of the pride and sense of honor of the American professional soldier. It is fashionable to denounce the military, and to ascribe to them a sinister and commanding influence over American policy. The truth that we ought to face is that the war in Vietnam was not made by the *military*, but by the *civilian* arm of government—and, for that matter, made by civilians within the executive (presidents, secretaries of state and defense, White House advisers) who regarded themselves as *liberal* men, not men of the right.

No doubt the military, through the joint chiefs of staff, contributed their naïve and optimistic estimates of the feasibility and ease of the American intervention. But they did not, in the last analysis, give the order to go. That order was given in the White House—and the inevitable result over nearly five grueling years has been the slow erosion of military morale, the breakdown of command authority, the deadly lapse into mindless and purposeless violence. Vietnam has been a tragedy for the American military because the old American sense of omnipotence has here been confronted by ample evidence of impotence: the result is a massive frustration and a disorientation of means—again the infamous free-fire zones, indiscriminate defoliation, random harassment and interdiction fire, and worst of all—massacre.

It is simply not true that such acts characterize all wars, or, as so alarmingly is held on the left, that such acts are hardly noteworthy since the entire war is an obscenity. To excuse My Lai or its like is simply to ignore the old medieval schoolman's entirely rational distinction between the morality *of* a war and the morality of conduct *in* that war. The philosophical distinction aside, such behavior on a large scale did not, as a matter of cold fact, characterize

American military operations in World War II or even in Korea.

But if the plight of the disheartened military counts for little to some people in the country, it is well to remember that many simple and fundamentally good men have been deceived about Vietnam and have selflessly died for it. Furthermore, there is simply the ultimate threat—or more accurately, the *further* threat—to American social stability that lies in the postwar reaction of this defeated military corps. Is it utter fancy to posit for these men the growth of that sullen legend of the "stab-in-the-back" dealt them by the civilian population that in Germany, after 1918, led to the growth of paramilitary reaction? It is difficult to see how one more disaffected social group in America can bode well for the future of our democracy.

One could go on and on. Poor America, its purposes discredited in the world, its reputation tarnished, its influence eroded, its society bloodied at home, its national myth of uniqueness broken, its population sullen and bewildered, its very commitment to democracy called into question—all for an ill-conceived folly begun with no thought of consequences more than a decade ago.

The War and the Economy

by Robert Eisner

1. *The Myth*

A stubborn myth haunts the nation: that the American economy in some sense "needs" the war in Indochina. Widespread among its opponents and a prop to proponents of our Southeast Asian venture, is the notion that prosperity depends upon war, and that peace will mean depression. Critics see economic interest in prolonging the war as a major obstacle to their efforts to end it. Supporters, particularly some trade union leaders, have even stressed publicly that millions of jobs are dependent upon our defense program.

The simple fact is that the war, with all its ramifications, is rapidly turning into a near disaster for the American economy.

The basis for the myth that the war sustains prosperity

Robert Eisner is professor of economics at Northwestern University and a member of the research staff of the National Bureau of Economic Research. He wrote Determinants of Capital Expenditures: An Interview Study *and* Some Factors in Growth Reconsidered, *and was co-author of "Determinants of Business Investment" in the* Commission on Money and Credit's Impacts of Monetary Policy.

The author is indebted to Gillian Hutchinson for assistance in preparing this paper, and also to William W. Kaufmann, Peter T. Knight, Ann Miller, Walter Oi, Mark Pauly and Larry Sjaastad for their aid and suggestions.

and that peace will bring depression is not hard to find. It goes back to many decades of experience with frequent if not chronic unemployment, culminating in the collapse of the 1930's. We were indeed finally pulled from the Great Depression by the outbreak of World War II.

It is true that if a burst of military or war spending is superimposed upon an economy with underemployment, the immediate effect is to give jobs to the unemployed. What is more, those previously unemployed spend their newly received incomes, as do their employers. These additional expenditures mean new income and jobs for the sellers and producers of the goods and services purchased; the "multiplier" makes its rounds.

By way of numerical illustration, imagine an economy with idle capacity in men and machines that could produce $90 billion per year in addition to current production. If the government suddenly begins to demand and order $30 billion worth of goods and services for war, these can be produced by drawing on one third of the idle capacity. Then, as the $30 billion of additional income are spent and respent, something in the order of the other $60 billion of idle capacity might eventually be put to use for production of the non-war goods which can be purchased out of increasing incomes.

2. *The Reality*

So much for the rationale of the myth. For that numerical illustration does not describe *this* war. Major escalation of our military role in Southeast Asia, beginning in 1965, took place against the backdrop of an economy near full employment.[1] Resources for war mainly had to come not from idle capacity but at the expense of non-war production. That expense had to come out of somebody's real, after-tax income. In fact, the cost came out of the real income of almost everybody: workers and businessmen, young and old, students and servicemen. Let none be fooled. The American economy as a whole is worse off by at least the more than $100 billion estimated to have been spent thus far in connection with our operations in Indochina. That some individuals have enjoyed "war profits," whether as investors, defense contractors, workers producing war material, or black market operators in Saigon, cannot obscure the total picture. If the economy as a whole has lost $100 billion, the arithmetic requirement that the whole equal the sum of its parts means that if some have gained, say, $50 billion, others must have lost $150 billion: $-100 = +50 - 150$.

This loss has been felt in a variety of ways, some the direct consequences of the war, some the less immediate results of governmental measures designed to cope with these consequences. The list of war costs reads like a catalog of evils and suffering in the American economy.

The war has caused inflation. The war has caused high taxes. The war has contributed to housing shortages. The war has drained resources in the areas of education, transportation, housing and all the services of government, from police protection to postal delivery. And the war and consequent inflation and government efforts to combat that inflation have now brought on the greatest stock-market crash since the thirties, the highest interest rates since the Civil War, falling production and rising unemployment.

Increases in prices and in taxes are easy to document. The consumer price index rose from 109.9 in 1965, when major military escalation began, to 134.4 in May 1970, an increase of 22.3 percent. Individual income-tax payments have risen by almost $45 billion, from $48.8 billion in the fiscal year 1965 to an estimated $92.2 billion in fiscal 1970, an increase of 89 percent, far more than the 50 percent increase in personal income over this period. The consequences of these sets of facts for real, after-tax incomes are easy to grasp.

TABLE 1. *Average Gross and Spendable Weekly Earnings*

| Year and Month | Manufacturing Industries | | | All Private Non-Agricultural Industries | | |
| | Current Prices | | Constant, March 1970 Prices* | Current Prices | | Constant, March 1970 Prices* |
	Gross	Spendable	Spendable	Gross	Spendable	Spendable
1965	$107.53	$ 96.78	$117.30	$ 95.06	$ 86.30	$104.60
1969	129.51	111.44	116.24	114.61	99.99	104.30
March 1970	132.40	114.85	114.85	117.92	103.39	103.39
Percent change, 1965 to March 1970	+23.1%	+18.7%	−2.1%	+24.0%	+19.8%	−1.2%

* Earnings in current prices multiplied by ratio of the March 1970 to current consumer price indices.

SOURCES: U.S. Department of Labor, Bureau of Labor Statistics, *Employment and Earnings* and *Economic Report of the President*.

Looking at average weekly earnings for production workers in manufacturing, for example, we see in Table 1 that these rose substantially in current prices, from $107.53 in 1965 to $132.40 in March 1970. But earnings in *real* terms, *after taxes*, showed no improvement over this five-year period. Indeed, converting to March 1970 prices, and taking account of the effects of inflation and taxes, the figures for average real *"spendable* earnings" * of a worker with three dependents go from $117.30 in 1965 to $114.85 in 1970, a drop of some 2 percent. The same measure for workers in all private nonagricultural industries shows a drop of 1.2 percent.

If a drop in real after-tax earnings of one or two percent does not seem large, one had better reflect on how sharply it contrasts with the long-term trend of rising income in

* Average gross weekly earnings, less social security and income taxes, worker with three dependents.

this most prosperous of nations. In the five-year period, 1960–65, prior to major war escalation, the average weekly spendable earnings of a worker with three dependents had increased 13.3 percent in manufacturing and just under 11 percent in all private non-agricultural industries. One might well have expected workers' real earnings to rise by another 10 or 11 percent in the five-year period 1965–70. In fact, there was actually a drop of 1 or 2 percent.

Many American workers are tense and angry at the frustrations of a society which seems to be drifting more and more into chaos. They have hardly been brought over in large numbers to the anti-war camp, let alone to the ranks of protesters. But though relatively few may see the basic cause, this palpable loss in real after-tax income must be a major factor in working-class malaise and tension.

Equally false is the illusion that while wage earners have suffered, corporate profits have soared. Rather, as noted by Louis B. Lundborg, chairman of the board of the Bank of America, the largest bank in the world, "During the four years prior to the escalation of the conflict in Vietnam, corporate profits after taxes rose 71.0 percent. From 1966 through 1969 corporate profits after taxes rose only 9.2 percent." [2] The calculations in Table 2 show that corporate profits have actually declined. From 1965 to the first quarter of 1970, corporate profits have declined by 11 percent. Accounting for inflation by putting these figures in first-quarter-1970 dollars, we see that after a rise of 61.2 percent from 1961 to 1965, real income in the form of profits has declined by 16.8 percent since escalation of the war beginning in 1965. (With population of course increasing, real *per capita* profits have actually declined significantly more.)

Individuals realize their corporate profits mainly in the form of capital gains on the stock that they own. Over many months, at every apparently significant rumor of moves toward peace—and many rumors not so significant

TABLE 2. *Corporate Profits*

Corporate Profits after Taxes

Period	Billions of Current Dollars	Billions of Constant, 1970-I, Dollars*
1961	$24.2	$34.4
1965	46.5	55.4
1969	50.5	52.1
1970-I	46.1	46.1
	Percent Changes	
1961 to 1965	+71.0%	+61.2%
1965 to 1969	+ 8.6%	− 6.0%
1965 to 1970-I	− 1.1%	−16.8%

* Using GNP implicit price deflator.

SOURCES: *Economic Report of the President* and *Survey of Current Business.*

—security prices soared. And at every dashing of peace hopes or expansion of the war, the market sagged again. (The stock market did indeed enjoy a substantial rise for a while, if one could forget the general inflation which canceled out most of the stock price increases over the 1966–68 period, as indicated in Table 3.)

But almost anyone from "middle America" can testify as well as an economist to what has happened as the war in Southeast Asia has dragged on. As this article is written, the financial markets are reeling from the shock of the Cambodian invasion, and stock prices are at their lowest level in more than seven years. After a *real* rise of 48.5 percent from the end of 1960 to the end of 1965, the real value of stocks has, as of May 26, 1970, declined almost $280 billion since the escalation year of 1965, a drop of 36.5 percent in constant dollars. And many additional billions have been lost in the value of bonds and other securities.

It may well be argued that the market suffers not from the war alone but from measures taken to combat inflation brought on by the war. There is certainly a measure of

TABLE 3. *Capital Gains and Losses*

Period	Initial Value of Holdings of Corporate Stock*	Gross Capital Gain	Net Capital Gain (Adjusted for Change in Real Value of Capital Stock)†	Net Capital Gain in Constant, 1970-I, Dollars	Net Gain as Percent of Initial Value, All in Constant, 1970-I, Dollars
			(Billions of Dollars)		
End of 1960 to End of 1965	$398.1	$238.4	$207.6	$244.6	+48.5%
End of 1965 to End of 1968	643.7	116.5	42.0	44.4	+ 5.9%
End of 1968 to 5/26/70	764.8	−277.6	−321.2	−321.2	−39.7%
End of 1965 to 5/26/70	643.7	−161.1	−276.6	−276.6	−36.5%

* Sum of holdings by households, institutions, mutual savings banks and private pension funds. Changes in the value of holdings from one period to the next are the sum of net acquisitions, not reported in this table, and gross capital gains, shown in the next column. Since net acquisitions (essentially purchases minus sales) are not generally zero, gross capital gains are not generally equal to the changes in value of holdings.

† GNP quarterly implicit price deflators used for adjustment. Stock indices used in end-of-year calculations are December and January means of daily closing averages.

SOURCES: Michael McElroy, *Capital Gains and the Theory and Measurement of Income*, Northwestern University doctoral dissertation, 1970, and special compilations by McElroy. Original data used in calculations taken from: Jean Crockett and Irwin Friend, "Characteristics of Stock Ownership," in *Proceedings of the Business and Economics Section*, American Statistical Association, 1963, pp. 146–68; Federal Reserve Board, *Flow of Funds Accounts, 1945–1967*, pp. 103–4; *Federal Reserve Bulletin*, May 1969, February 1970; *National Income and Product Accounts of the United States, 1929–1965*; *Survey of Current Business*, April 1970; Standard and Poor's 500 Stock Index, and the New York Stock Exchange Index.

truth to this. Costs of the war have in fact been met by both inflation and higher taxes. The higher taxes, on corporate profits, tax surcharges, and abandonment of the investment tax credit, have directly reduced business earnings and the expectation of future business earnings. But further, the extremely high rates of interest, brought on by inflation and resulting tight-money policies, mean a greater rate of discount for expected future earnings, whether from bonds or stock, and lower prices for both.

Resources have been drained to finance the war, and almost nowhere has the impact been more sharply felt than in housing. The combination of inflation, tight money and existing financial institutions has priced much of possible new construction out of today's market. Increases in costs of land, labor and materials have been notorious, running to 10 percent, by one estimate, from 1968 to 1969 alone. But the high interest rates, a product of both inflation and the efforts to check inflation with tight money, have themselves paradoxically raised the cost and reduced the availability of housing.

The huge rise in interest rates has brought corresponding increases in monthly payments on mortgage loans. For example, the rise in mortgage rates from approximately 5.5 percent in 1965 to some 8.4 percent in 1970 means that monthly payments on a new twenty-year loan have risen by 25.4 percent. Over the full life of a twenty-year $20,000 mortgage, the increased rates mean increased payments of $8,491. And even this is only part of the story. In fact, mortgage loans are difficult to get, and many would-be borrowers who might have obtained money under pre-war conditions cannot obtain loans now.

In real terms, housing progress or lack of it may be measured in the number of "starts," that is, the number of housing units on which construction has commenced. In February of 1968, President Johnson called for construction over the next ten years of 26 million new housing units, which have been translated into 2.6 million units per year. Average non-farm housing starts from 1960 to 1966 had been only 1.4 million units per year. In 1967 the figure was down to 1.3 million units. By December 1969, starts were down to an annual rate of 1.245 million units and by April 1970 to 1.18 million. It has been pre-

dicted that starts on single-family homes will probably
decline 14 percent in 1970 and rental-apartment construction by 19 percent. In the face of great need, a need recognized as being at the core of serious social problems, we
have fallen further and further behind in this war economy.

Failure to construct needed housing now is not only a
current cost but a cost for the future as well. Indeed,
financing a war by deferring investment of any kind is a
way of passing the real cost of the war on to a "future
generation," which will lack the capital goods—in this
case, houses—that should have been constructed now. The
housing shortages to which we have been contributing
during these war years, and to which we are continuing
to contribute, will plague us for years and decades to come.

Housing is one of the prime sectors to have suffered
from the draining of resources to war. It is certainly not
the only one. A whole generation, particularly in urban
ghettos, is growing up without adequate education. Public
schools, faced with overcrowding, inadequate facilities, insufficient and relatively inexperienced staffs, and overwhelming neighborhood problems, have in many instances
virtually given up educational efforts.

Problems of urban and suburban transport have become
critical. We are choked in our own cars and exhaust
fumes. The solution of our difficulties would take money
and resources. These resources have been devoted to war
in a profligate fashion, but not to the pressing problems
of peace.

3. Total Dollar Costs of the War

Budget costs of the Vietnam war, derived from estimates
of the Defense Comptroller, are given in Table 4. They
total 104.9 billion current dollars and 113.4 billion fiscal-
year-1970 dollars, reaching a peak annual rate in the
neighborhood of $30 billion[3] in fiscal year 1969.

Large as they are, these costs are only the expenditures

TABLE 4. *Budget Costs of the Vietnam War in Current and Fiscal Year 1970 Dollars*
Fiscal Years 1966–1970

Fiscal Year	Billions of Current Dollars	Billions of FY 1970 Dollars
1966	5.8	6.8
1967	20.1	23.1
1968	26.5	29.6
1969	28.8	30.7
1970	23.2	23.2
Five-Year Total	104.9	113.4

SOURCE: *Economic Costs of the Second Indochinese War to the American Citizen*, a background paper prepared by Peter T. Knight of the Brookings Institution. Some of the information in this table is also presented in Charles L. Schultze, *Setting National Priorities, The 1971 Budget* (Brookings, 1970), Table 2-12, p. 48.

paid out by the U.S. Treasury. Actual costs to the economy are in fact much more. A first major addition relates to the true cost of those of our armed forces for which we do not pay a market price, but which we rather draft at remuneration far below even the minimum wages set in civilian work. One very conservative measure of this added cost comes from *The Report of the President's Commission on an All-Volunteer Armed Force.* The commission estimates that shifting to an all-volunteer force by July 1, 1971, apparently presuming a substantial de-escalation of the Vietnam conflict and reduction of total armed forces by that date, would imply a net cost to the Treasury of $2.7 billion. The larger forces involved in the major military activity in which we have thus far been engaged must clearly cost considerably more.

The true cost of a soldier or a sailor or a marine is not what we pay him when he is drafted or is a "reluctant volunteer" to avoid the draft. It is rather what we would have to pay him if he was not *forced* to serve. This indeed measures not merely a cost of the war in terms of psychological aversion on the part of its participants but an economic cost in terms of incomes they would be earning—

the goods and services they would be producing—if they were civilians.

There are other usually unmeasured costs of the war and the means, including the draft, by which it has been prosecuted. How many hundreds of thousands of young men have been wasting years in colleges that they do not wish to attend, and wasting educational resources which they do not want and do not use, because they find this the most effective means of avoiding service in a war of which they want no part? How many young men have been forced into idleness or temporary jobs because employers would not hire them in view of the possible imminence of military service? How many indeed have left the economy by literally hiding from the draft, fleeing the country or going to prison? At least some of these costs of conscription attributable to the Vietnam war are indicated in Table 5.

TABLE 5. *Estimates of Added Economic Costs of Conscription**

Fiscal Year (Ending June 30)	Average Armed Forces, Millions of Men	Added Costs of Conscription, Billions of Dollars, 1970
1966	2,870	2.9
1967	3,344	13.9
1968	3,483	19.5
1969	3,534	21.8
1970	3,456 (est.)	18.3

* The Appendix at the end of this chapter explains the derivation of these estimates.

On a macabre note, one must also measure the lost earnings of our war casualties. There were 50,866 American deaths of all causes in the Vietnam theater as of June 20, 1970. In addition, there were 142,117 injuries requiring hospitalization and 139,584 injuries not requiring hospitalization.[4] Vietnam-era recipients of service-connected disability compensation totaled 145,008.[5] The mean disability rate of these recipients is 35.5 percent.[6]

Fifty thousand Americans who have died in Southeast Asia might have produced $20 billion worth of goods and services over their lifetimes. It might be argued that some of this would have been used for their own support, but a significant portion certainly would have gone to support wives and children and society as a whole. Several hundred thousand wounded will have their economic productivity impaired for weeks or months or years or all of their lives. Many of them will require costly medical care long after the war is over. Here are uncounted billions of dollars of war costs rarely measured in conventional accounting.

In dollars of fiscal-year-1970 purchasing power, budgetary expenses come to $113.4 billion. The added cost of conscription is another $76.4 billion. Costs of the dead and wounded, calculated by discounting to the present some detailed estimates of the lost incomes they might have earned, are put at $23.1 billion.[7] Total costs come finally to $212.9 billion.

How can one comprehend such a staggering total? To what is it equivalent in dwelling units for our people, in classrooms for our children, in police protection, in medical research, in foreign aid for peaceful development?

And yet the war and measures to cope with it have had still other indirect costs. At the moment, in the midst of one of the worst inflations in our history, we are also suffering a rise in unemployment and decrease in production. The nation's unemployment rose from 4.4 to 4.8 percent of the civilian labor force in April 1970, the sharpest rise in ten years, and rose further, to 5.0 percent in May. The real rate of Gross National Product declined for two successive quarters and personal income in May 1970 showed the largest monthly drop ever recorded (from $801.3 billion to $793.5 billion, with special factors contributing, however, to the high April figure). All this is clearly accountable to measures taken to counteract war-induced inflation.

Whatever the vagaries of reflection of war costs upon the economy in the nation, we face one underlying fact. There is a real loss in the diversion of resources of men and capital, of the capital not constructed because of the production for war, of the lives ruined and destroyed because of the war. The best-laid plans of economists in the way of tax policy or monetary policy can merely reduce the magnification of these losses and costs.

In their original magnitude the costs are real and inescapable. But these costs are just our own. We have said nothing in this discussion about the economic loss and ravished earth and destroyed capital and men, women and children in the land on which we fight.

NOTES

1. The unemployment rate averaged 4.5 percent in 1965 and in January 1966 stood at 4.0 percent, the figure widely taken as corresponding to "full employment." The rate later dipped further, to 3.3 percent in December 1968, but rose to 5 percent by May 1970, with widespread predictions that unemployment will rise still more before the year is out.

2. Testimony before Senate Committee on Foreign Relations, April 15, 1970, p. 7.

3. This may be contrasted with the estimate of $23 billion for peak *incremental* outlay for the war, presented by Charles L. Schultze, former Budget Director under President Johnson. With total military expenditures for goods and services in the neighborhood of seventy and eighty billion dollars per year, it may indeed be difficult to know how much was properly accounted or should properly be accounted to Vietnam. A portion of the war budget might conceivably have been spent in maintaining troops in garrison or in peaceful maneuvers of ships and planes if there had been no war. Some suggest that other defense expenditures have been cut in order to free resources or dollars for Vietnam. But others may well argue that the war has contributed to a climate both at home and abroad that has made total non-war defense expenditures more than they might otherwise have been.

4. From Department of Defense *Weekly Southeast Asia Casualty Summary*.

5. From Information Service of Veterans Administration, *Statistical Summary of VA Activities*, March 1970.

6. Calculated from *Statistical Supplement to 1969 Annual Report,* Administrator of Veterans Affairs, Table 15, p. 11.

7. The economic cost of the dead is in one sense overstated by failing to net out the added consumption costs if they had lived. On the other hand, data to estimate future costs of medical and nursing care for the wounded are not available and these costs have been omitted. At the very rough level of approximation of these estimates, the two omissions may be taken as mutually offsetting.

APPENDIX: ADDED CONSCRIPTIVE COSTS

Added costs of conscription are estimated from the cubic equation ACC = $-52.93 + 71.12$ AF $-31.24(AF)^*$ + 4.64 (AF),† doubled to allow for what Dr. Larry Sjaastad, who was in charge of research on "The Conscription Tax," for *The Report of the President's Commission on an All-Volunteer Armed Force*** calls collection costs." These are the costs to the economy of actions to avoid the draft, such as prolongation of student status and uneconomic occupational choice, as well as other, extra nonmilitary costs related to the draft. Finally, to arrive at the figures in Table 5, we then subtract $4.24 billion per year, an amount equal to the added costs we would have had from conscription even if we had not been in Vietnam. Non-Vietnam, added costs of conscription are taken as the cost of maintaining armed forces of 2,500,000. This number corresponds roughly to the 2,482,000 personnel on duty as of June 30, 1961, or the 2,685,000 of June 30, 1964, after the latter figure is adjusted for the 21,000 then actually in Vietnam* and a reasonable allowance for the added forces at home which must have been associated in one capacity or another with those already in the Southeast Asia theater of operations or soon to be deployed there. It should be noted that this may well cause a decided underestimate of conscription costs attributable to the war.† A strong argument can be made that in the absence of growing involvement in Indochina throughout the 1960's, conscrip-

---

* Data taken from *The Budget of the United States Government for the Fiscal Year Ending June 30, 1966* (United States Government Printing Office, 1965), p. 70, and *Budget of the United States Government: Fiscal Year 1969* (United States Government Printing Office, 1968), p. 13.

† An earlier version of this paper presented to the Joint Economic Committee's Subcommittee on Government Economy, and using a quadratic instead of a cubic equation, made no such subtraction.

** United States Government Printing Office, Washington, February 1970.

tion would have been abandoned or, at least, actual draft calls would have shrunk to zero as there would have been an adequate supply of true volunteers for a small peacetime army.

The cubic equation was calculated from the Commission estimates of added budgetary expenses in 1970 dollars of $1.47 billion, $1.74 billion, $2.12 billion, and $4.55 billion required to maintain fully voluntary forces of 2 million, 2.25 million, 2.5 million, and 3.0 million men respectively.‡ Estimates of added budgetary costs of a volunteer armed force are measures of the "conscription tax," the serviceman's evaluation of that part of the value of his military service for which he is not paid when he is drafted. The "conscription tax" is adjusted, as noted above, so as to reflect only the *incremental* costs of maintaining more than the 2,500,000 "normal" peacetime force.

Estimates of the cost of an all-volunteer force made by the Department of Defense in 1966, discussed in Appendix C of *The Report of the President's Commission*, it may be noted, are much higher, ranging from $5.51 billion to $16.66 billion for armed forces of only 2.7 million with an unemployment rate of 4.0 percent, which would be consistent with our analysis. Both the DOD and Commission estimates assume a situation of peace. In abstracting from the cost of inducing volunteers to participate in this particular war and to accept the risk of combat in it, both sets of estimates would clearly understate the hypothetical cost of current wartime recruitment of volunteers. They may not be so low, however, as a measure of the "opportunity cost" of military service, the extra earnings which conscripts might have received as civilians. We have worked from the lower Commission estimates to have a conservative set of projections.

The Sjaastad estimates of "collection costs" of the "conscription tax," in the neighborhood of 1.5 times the tax, were derived indirectly from a probability model of the incidence of service and the costs to the economy of all those whose economic activity is affected by the possibility of being drafted. We have applied a ratio of only 1.0 in order to reflect the greater incidence of service in the larger wartime armed forces and in order, again, to have conservative estimates.

‡ *The Report of the President's Commission*, pp. 189–92 (Tables A-VIII through A-XI).

A Program for Disengagement

by George McGovern

AN AMERICAN disengagement from the bloody, senseless war in Indochina will provide no panacea for all the problems of either the Vietnamese or American societies, but it is a clear prerequisite for their solution. The alternative is more death and devastation for the people of Southeast Asia, more violence and disorder in our own society, more damage to our own economy, and more erosion of our material and spiritual strength as we waste on war what we need to fight crises at home.

In official statements the administration has repeatedly spoken of its desire for withdrawal, seemingly cognizant of the delusion of trying to achieve military victory in Vietnam. One lesson that we all should have learned from our past blunders, however, is how rapidly the best stated intentions are destroyed by contradictory actions. American military involvement in Vietnam cannot be ended by expanding the area of the war any more than withdrawal

The Honorable George McGovern, U.S. Senator from South Dakota since 1962, was a member of the U.S. House of Representatives (1958–61) and special assistant to the President and director of Food for Peace (1961–62). He has a Ph.D. from Northwestern University and was professor of history and government at Dakota Wesleyan University. He was awarded the Distinguished Flying Cross as a bomber pilot in World War II.

can be accomplished by latching it to conditions beyond our control.

For many—members of Congress and others—the invasion of Cambodia last April was the final straw. The same mindless killing which has plagued Vietnam for years was suddenly inflicted on hapless Cambodian peasants. This invasion, no matter how it is couched in euphemisms, displayed a contempt for the processes called for under the Constitution. It sent American forces across an international border, into a neutral country, without a request from that country, in disregard of both international and domestic law. It was done without even informal consultations with Congress. These steps gave us a few easily replaceable enemy supplies, but they brought us a wider war.

The President's decision to invade Cambodia was, in the words of former Secretary of Defense Clark Clifford, "taking our nation down a road that is leading us more deeply into Vietnam rather than taking us out."

Only ten days before the invasion of Cambodia, President Nixon announced plans to withdraw 150,000 more combat troops from Vietnam by June 1971, which works out to be the same monthly rate he used during the previous year. Formerly the euphoria at the sound of the word "withdrawal" had clouded discussion of the actual policy being pursued, but no longer. Now there is an increasing public awareness that the President has never committed himself to withdrawing all American forces from Vietnam. Upon conclusion of his schedule next year, some 285,000 Americans still will remain in the Vietnamese quagmire.

And successful implementation of even the trickling withdrawal rate announced by President Nixon is itself subject to three conditions he first enunciated on November 3: progress at Paris, the ability of the South Vietnamese to fill in the gaps left by the American withdrawal and a low level of activity by the North Vietnamese and Viet-Cong. Progress at the Paris peace talks appears to be minimal at this juncture.

The other two criteria effectively take the decision-making out of our own hands and force us to react to the actions of Saigon and Hanoi rather than initiate policy on the basis of our own interests. As long as President Thieu has such power over American policy, there is no end in sight for our military involvement in Indochina.

This is no time for an ambivalent policy—a policy which, at best, only allows us to extricate ourselves from Vietnam if and when uncontrollable conditions are fulfilled; a policy which in the end promises us a deeper involvement in Southeast Asia. We need a clear, unequivocal policy which will lead to a systematic termination of our involvement in the war.

The essentials of such a policy have been embodied in Amendment 609, the "Amendment to End the War." At this writing the amendment has not been voted on, but regardless of the result, two key issues presented by Amendment 609 will be significant in the ongoing debate about American policy in Indochina: (1) a substantive program for disengagement from Indochina, (2) congressional assertion of its Constitutional prerogatives.

Through the "Amendment to End the War," Congress has at long last shown itself to be willing to *share* the responsibility and the risk of taking decisive action with regard to Vietnam. If the President is fearful of the political consequences of ending the war by withdrawing our forces, this amendment counters: "Mr. President, we are now going to share that risk with you." In my view our Constitutional system gives Congress that obligation.

Amendment 609 presents a program for withdrawal which punctuates the urgency and necessity of an orderly American disengagement. It sets out the sort of unequivocal policy needed to bring to a close this sad episode in American history.

The operative provisions establish that

> *no part of any funds appropriated pursuant to this Act or
> any other law shall be expended in Vietnam after De-
> cember 1970, for any purpose arising from military conflict;*
> Provided that, funds may be expended as required for the
> safe and systematic withdrawal of all United States military
> personnel, the termination of United States military oper-
> ations, the provision of assistance to South Vietnam in
> amounts and for purposes specifically authorized by the
> Congress, the exchange of prisoners, and the arrangement
> of asylum for Vietnamese who might be physically endan-
> gered by the withdrawal of all United States forces, and
> Further Provided, *that the withdrawal of all United States
> military personnel from Vietnam shall be completed no
> later than June 30, 1971,* unless the Congress, by joint reso-
> lution, approves a finding by the President that an addi-
> tional stated period of time is required to insure the safety
> of such personnel during the withdrawal process. [Emphasis
> added.]

These points recognize both our commitments and responsibilities as well as our primary interest—withdrawing our young men from the civil strife of Southeast Asia.
Other proposals of the same nature have been made by
Clark Clifford, who advocates a publicly announced, rapid-
withdrawal timetable, and by other analysts.* Although
there are some slight differences in timing between the
schedule written into the "Amendment to End the War"
and Mr. Clifford's three-point proposal detailed in the
May 22 issue of *Life,* the basic thrust is the same: to establish an irreversible program, or timetable, for withdrawal.

An effective program for disengagement has three essential requisites: (1) a total withdrawal of American
forces, (2) an announced end date for the completion of
withdrawal, and (3) completion of withdrawal at an early
time.

---

* An excellent analysis of the reasons for a timetable was presented by
Les Gelb and Morton H. Halperin in the Washington *Post,* May 23, 1970.

Total Withdrawal

Our timetable proposes cutting off funds after a specified date (in this case, December 1970) "for any purpose arising from military conflict" in Vietnam except for amounts required for a "safe and systematic withdrawal of all United States military personnel" and "the termination of United States military operations." All our troops, combat and support alike, will be withdrawn.

The President has at most only committed himself to the withdrawal of American combat troops from Vietnam. This policy of splitting off our combat forces and leaving the relatively defenseless support troops sitting on their bases is a dangerous flirtation with disaster and/or re-escalation.

Under the President's projected schedule the protection of the 285,000 American troops left in Vietnam after June 1971 will rest primarily on the shaky shoulders of the "Vietnamized" Army of the Republic of Vietnam (ARVN), a force now apparently more interested in neighboring Cambodia than in its own country. If the ARVN proved incapable or unwilling to meet their responsibilities—very real possibilities—there would be powerful pressures on President Nixon to reintroduce large numbers of American combat troops into Vietnam or take even tougher measures.

In April 1970, the President argued that sanctuaries which had existed in the Cambodian jungle for a full five years were suddenly a threat to our fighting men. That presumed threat was met by an invasion. Strangely, while Mr. Nixon was telling us that the enemy had to be attacked because of a build-up of the border sanctuaries, Secretary of Defense Melvin Laird was explaining that the attack was launched because enemy forces were moving *away* from the border, thus assuring us fewer casualties. At any rate, after the invasion of Cambodia there is cer-

tainly no reason to doubt that the President's future reactions—especially if faced with a real threat—would go
the route of escalation.

In fact, the President has made his thoughts about escalation very clear. At a press conference on April 20, 1970,
Mr. Nixon distinguished his own path from the escalation
followed by President Johnson:

> . . . the difference is that he [Johnson] did move step by
> step. This action is a decisive move, and this action also
> puts the enemy on warning that if it escalates while we are
> trying to de-escalate, we will move decisively and not step
> by step.

To avoid the danger of placing the United States in a
position where re-escalation might appear the only way to
save American lives, it is absolutely necessary to withdraw
all American forces from Vietnam.

Announced End Date

Our timetable calls for the completion of the "withdrawal of all United States military personnel from Viet
nam" no later than June 30, 1971. This clear signal that
the United States is really leaving Indochina can surmount
several major impediments to peace.

The likely first consequence of such a timetable will be
progress toward at least an informal end of hostilities between U.S. and enemy forces. Under the Vietnamization
strategy the other side has an uninterrupted incentive to
attack Americans remaining in Vietnam. In their view,
each of our men is a potent combat threat who will stay,
or whose replacement will stay, many years into the future.

The timetable will reverse that incentive. Its terms
provide, in fact, that the deadline for complete withdrawal may be extended by joint resolution if Congress
finds that all U.S. manpower cannot be withdrawn safely
by that time. This is unmistakable notice to the adversary

that any assaults against American forces risk a longer U.S. presence. Thus, the timetable formula offers far greater security for our troops than the current Vietnamization procedure.

The timetable might also break the deadlock in Paris, where negotiators have done little more than exchange invectives for many months. The central dispute there is the composition of the Saigon government, which is what the Vietnamese civil war is all about. The offer of elections is hollow when viewed from the other side because we insist that the Thieu–Ky regime must be in charge of all governmental machinery, including the administration of elections—until they are held. Our proposal for mutual withdrawals is illusory for the same reason. Thus the talks are stalemated, and the President's policy, not unlike his predecessor's, can only rest on the vain hope that military action—with perhaps more "decisive" moves in store—can pressure the North Vietnamese and the NLF to accept our position.

Establishing a timetable leaves open the extent of U.S. assistance, short of manpower, to South Vietnam as an extremely important bargaining issue. It also adds a new element. By laying out a definite date for an end to the involvement of U.S. manpower, it will encourage the Thieu-Ky government toward a more accommodating position at the same time that it will pressure the other side to negotiate while the United States, always more conciliatory than our Saigon allies, still has a direct battlefield interest.

A fixed timetable will also have a desirable effect on Saigon. Present policy makes the removal of U.S. forces contingent on the strength of the South Vietnamese; in effect, it makes us captives of Messrs. Thieu and Ky. If they want us to stay, as they do since their very claim to power is based upon our guarantee, they need only to display their own weaknesses and threaten their own collapse. So long as we remain in this curious posture we give Thieu and Ky a motive to resist the political and economic reforms which are essential if they are to survive past our departure. We invite them to abuse our help.

If the existing Saigon government is ever to be viable and self-sufficient, it needs an unmistakable statement, established in law, that after a fixed time U.S. forces will no longer be available as guarantors of its power. Far from abandoning allies, this timetable may well rescue the South Vietnamese from the repression of their own government by giving that government an incentive to reform itself and to include groups thus far excluded from political processes.

Early Completion of Withdrawal

Administration spokesmen have stated frequently that Vietnamization is similar to this timetable in that it, too, contemplates turning the war over to the South Vietnamese. But they argue strenuously against a definite plan.

In the President's November 3 speech he made it appear that the United States has only two roads out of Vietnam: (1) his approach, and (2) what he caricatures as "precipitous withdrawal." Although that term has never been defined in terms of months, years or decades it is apparently intended to describe any approach that would move faster than the President is willing to go. In fact, the proponents of a program for total disengagement are not advocating anything that could be termed "precipitous"—the timetable in Amendment 609 provides for withdrawal by July 1971, hardly a reckless pace. It is a timetable that any competent commander could meet in a systematic and orderly fashion.

Beyond this, the administration has tried to deflect the public debate from the question of time to the question of the effects of U.S. withdrawal. The most prominent argument is the "bloodbath" prognosis, the concept that if we pull out of Vietnam "millions" of South Vietnamese —to use the President's most recent estimate—will be butchered.

Such expressions of concern must be viewed with bitter irony by the hundreds of thousands of Vietnamese civilians who have found themselves in the midst of our chosen battlefield. The victims of saturation bombing, free-fire zones, and the like—running to some 4,300 civilian casualties each month, by conservative estimates —know that there is a terrible bloodbath going on now.

Beyond that, the "historical" foundation of the bloodbath argument—North Vietnam after 1954 and Hue during the 1968 Tet offensive—has been well researched by scholars and informed observers, and found wanting. No one can deny the possibility of harsh retribution after the war. But it is a possibility no matter who prevails, and if it is a threat, continued futile warfare is unlikely to prevent it. A far better solution is to provide asylum in friendly countries for those individual Vietnamese who feel that our withdrawal would place them in personal danger.

Moreover, on a more substantive level, the entire bloodbath thesis rests upon a faulty premise. As Gelb and Halperin wrote in the May 23 issue of the Washington *Post,* "the interesting thing about the bloodbath argument is that it must hide either the belief that the South Vietnamese army is worthless and hopeless or the conviction that U.S. forces can never be fully withdrawn—or both." Withdrawal will leave South Vietnam with ARVN and national police forces totaling at least 1,100,000 men, all equipped with the finest weapons American technology and American money can supply. Viet-Cong and North Vietnamese forces in the South number no more than 200,000, with another 400,000 North Vietnamese not committed to battle. The numerical superiority of the South is further augmented by forces from other Southeast Asian nations. To be sure, the South Vietnamese will be unable to win a military victory after our troops are gone. Their forces and ours combined have been unable to do that. But it is nonsense to suggest that the entire country will quickly fall to the Communists after we have left, unless South Vietnamese forces are so ill-motivated and disinterested—still, after all these years of help—that they will not even have the capacity for self-defense.

In either case, the only result to be gained from prolonged U.S. presence in Vietnam is more American casualties in a futile cause.

In sum, the administration has argued that the costs of a program for rapid withdrawal from Vietnam are greater than the costs of staying. As this and other essays in this book have shown, the opposite is the case.

A program for disengagement as presented in Amendment 609 will prevent deeper involvement and re-escalation of the conflict. It will free the President from military pressure to reduce or reverse the withdrawal process. It will stop the growth of tragically long lists of American dead and wounded, and will redirect the attention of our government to the homeland, where the solution of enormous problems requires a concerted effort by all Americans. And it will allow conflicting military and political forces in Vietnam to seek their own level free of the heavy, unnatural pressure we have applied.

The costs of remaining the captive of a mistaken policy are too great, and the probable gains are near worthless—or worse. It is time to end cheap talk about the United States becoming a "second-rate power" or a "pitiful, helpless giant." It is time to abandon a policy of saving face and to institute a policy of saving lives.

Humility Yes, Humiliation No:
The Need for a New World-View

by Seyom Brown

DEFEAT IS COSTLY. But there comes a time when persistence in the pursuit of an illusory victory or an impractical stalemate becomes even more costly. One has then to begin to think seriously about absorbing the costs of defeat.

The Nixon administration gives no sign of having reached the point of realizing that acceptance of defeat in Vietnam is the least costly of a set of bad alternatives. If and when official Washington does reach this point, it would be compounding the folly of intervention to exaggerate the international consequences of a complete and rapid withdrawal of U.S. combat troops, support troops, and air support—even though this paves the way for a complete Communist take-over of Vietnam. A U.S. withdrawal under such circumstances would be a defeat (however we might dress it up), and it would be wise to recognize it as such—not a "humiliating" defeat of the United States and everything it stands for, but a defeat of a set of particular objectives and an obsolete world-view.

Since such a defeat may well be the only alternative to

Seyom Brown was a political analyst at the RAND Corporation, Santa Monica, California, from 1962 to 1969. He is the author of The Faces of Power: Constancy and Change in United States Foreign Policy from Truman to Johnson.

an open-ended American military involvement, it is prudent to ask how to bring it off at the least cost, and how to live with it—even, perhaps, how to transmute it into a creative opportunity.

If the administration finally is persuaded that rapid and complete U.S. military withdrawal is the least costly alternative viewed in terms of the situations in Vietnam and within the United States, the question will still be asked: What of our international position, our status as a great power, our reputation for fulfilling our commitments, our word? Will the credit attached to U.S. undertakings all over the world be so undermined by a defeat in Vietnam that our web of alliances will crumble? Will our adversaries and the adversaries of our allies be encouraged to engage in provocations previously deterred by their fear of U.S. counteraction?

Just as there are dangers in exaggerating our defeat in Vietnam, there are dangers in viewing it as simply a tactical defeat. The policies which have caused our intervention and defeat in Southeast Asia stem from a world-view inappropriate to the complexities of international relations in the last third of the twentieth century. If we do not translate what is now happening in Southeast Asia into an opportunity to reformulate our world-view, we risk repeating the Vietnam experience or even perpetuating worse disasters.

The primary task, then, in reducing the international damage we are bound to bear from Vietnam is to divest ourselves of a set of interrelated notions: (1) that the United States has a responsibility for redressing imbalances of power in Asia that place anti-Communist elements at a disadvantage in opposition to Communist elements; (2) that the United States has direct peace-keeping functions in Asia apart from the protection of our own citizens, facilities, lines of communication and transport, and rights of passage; (3) that the United States has a special political-mentor function in Asia, as elsewhere, having in our wisdom and organizational ability developed a constitutional system suited to the nature of man; (4) that the United States is specially qualified to direct and participate in the process of economic development in the area; and (5) that the United States is the essential and dominant sponsor and planner of regional multilateral economic and security institutions for Asia.

Delusion 1: The U.S. as Redresser of the Balance

The delusion that the United States has been specially called by the god of history to protect weak anti-Communists from strong Communists has contributed in large measure to bringing on those very situations we purportedly seek to avert: weak anti-Communists and strengthened Communist fronts in various countries, "requiring" our continued assistance to redress the imbalance. To continue policies based on the assumption of our indispensability to a balance of power in Southeast Asia will mean that we continue to play favorites, supporting clients on the basis of our shared fear of Asian Communism and China.

We will continue to provide anti-regime elements in the anti-Communist Southeast Asian countries with the rallying cry that the incumbent regimes are a part of a U.S.-organized, neo-colonial alliance system meant to resist radical change, and thereby will perpetuate the fiction that the real champions of progressive social change are the Communist parties and the Communist nations.

Such anti-Communist policies by the United States will continue to provide Asian parties of the left (Marxist and non-Marxist) with a rationale for accepting tutelage, help —possibly even direct military assistance—from the Communist nations in order to redress perceived imbalances of forces against the left.

It will perpetuate situations in Southeast Asia that

tempt political intervention by the Communist nations in the internal affairs of other countries. This intervention can easily expand into overt paramilitary participation when political conflict becomes civil war, and may then become indistinguishable from "aggression" across borders, activating further U.S. collective-security obligations.

This cycle of self-confirming fears of Communist intervention lies at the base of our existing commitments and interventions in Southeast Asia. Without breaking this delusional chain, no U.S. administration will be able to give operation to the principle in President Nixon's State of the World message, that our commitments ought to flow from our basic interests. In practice we will continue to invest commitments—merely because they are commitments—with so much prestige that they become, willy-nilly, "vital" interests in their own right.

Unless the United States government now begins to divest itself of these prestige-inflated interests and commitments in Southeast Asia (and other regions) and soberly reevaluates American basic interests, a failure to fulfill our "obligation" to keep South Vietnam from coming under Communist control will indeed call into serious question *all* solemn foreign obligations of the United States.

Delusion 2: The United States as Guardian of the Peace

The assumption of a special and weighty U.S. peace-keeping role in Asia—increasingly advanced these days as a fall-back position for maintaining our involvement without the standard Cold War balance-of-power rationale—is also subject to damaging pitfalls.

Painful as it is to admit, direct U.S. participation in peace-keeping ventures is the surest way to contaminate them as disguised perpetuations of the U.S. politico-military presence. The function of international peace-keeping efforts should be to depolarize and thereby defuse a local belligerency. This can only be accomplished through injecting a third "neutral" presence symbolizing the interest of the world community against further bloodshed and dangerous escalation. The Cyprus and Congo peacekeeping activities by the United Nations, though far from tidy in their operation and outcome, provide useful models. The United States has temporarily lost its claim to represent the world interest in the quarantine of local conflicts. It is only through a new record of self-restraint internationally that we can earn the acceptance, once again, of the United States as an agent for peace.

Delusion 3: The United States as Political Tutor

Even more painful perhaps is the need to recognize that the principles of liberal democracy may not be exportable, and are certainly not suitable to be carried directly into another country by Americans, as if political systems were objects to be tinkered with out of our technical-assistance toolbox. If our defeat in Vietnam is interpreted by liberals to be the result of insufficient early stress by the United States on political reform and simply an overapplication of military power, if they do not realize that psycho-cultural violence can be inflicted on other cultures by insisting on our way of structuring socio-political relationships through the ballot and Western-style political parties, then the American policy community will sooner or later self-righteously lead the country into another Big Muddy.

Delusion 4: The United States as Economic Benefactor

We have been so convinced that we are doing good work in the world that we have become oblivious to the effects of our noble intentions. Our economic-assistance programs have suffered from this hubris no less than our political reform and our explicit counter-insurgency programs.

Assistance to provide the government of a developing country with the resources necessary to pursue projects of social reconstruction and economic modernization has some chance of success where the recipient government is highly dedicated to these goals and is generally respected by broad segments of the population. But many governments receiving U.S. development assistance do not fulfill either of these criteria. Rather, the injection of U.S. economic resources frequently ends up in sophisticated weapons and glamorous uniforms for the military— bakshish for their suppression of opposition movements and/or payoffs to restrain the military from attempting to take over the government themselves. To assure against the misuse of development aid by politically insecure and corrupt regimes, the United States must meddle in the internal politics of the recipient country, attaching "strings" which embarrass nationalist leaders and undermine their popular support even further, and finally failing to contribute to development goals.

In Southeast Asia, corruption and political illegitimacy have been winked at by the United States in dispensing economic assistance. With the priority objective being the suppression of Communist insurgency, economic assistance has been given as a part of a total counter-insurgency package, without too many questions asked. This is particularly true in Vietnam, where the aid is essentially an adjunct to a full-blown war effort.

As an instrument of counter-insurgency, economic assistance becomes, in effect, blood money—enhancing the lethal capabilities of certain segments of the population against others. Throughout the region, this is the role we have assumed: the benefactor not of development but of particular factions in the civil strife of countries whose social systems we do not adequately understand.

Delusion 5: The United States as Regional Impresario

The notion that the United States can lessen its own risks and embarrassments through the construction of localized mutual-security pacts among "reliable" anti-Communist regimes—whether ostensibly associations to further economic and political development or to cooperate in putting down subversion—has the same faults today as it did when it was championed by John Foster Dulles. In the first place, most regimes in Southeast Asia, whatever the personal rectitude of their officials, have very shallow roots in shifting local politics. The "ins" today may be the "outs" tomorrow; and contending factions will often exploit regional ethnic animosities against neighboring countries in order to mobilize domestic political support.

Secondly, the use of anti-Communism, or the fear of Chinese or North Vietnamese expansion, as a means of gaining cohesion among such disparate regimes only serves to perpetuate the polarization of the region and the polarization of indigenous politics—leading again to the chain reactions that tempt overcommitment and intervention by the superpowers.

It will take considerable time before any direct U.S. assistance to Southeast Asia will be free from the polarizing stigma of anti-Communism, whether funds are funneled through bilateral channels or the regional multilateral associations we are now trying to sponsor as spin-offs from the Southeast Asia Treaty Organization (SEATO). To reduce the divisive harm of U.S.-sponsored anti-Communism, we will have to revamp completely the objectives and institutional modalities of our assistance to the area.

The first step, then, will be to divest ourselves of the obsolete world-view that has produced the Vietnam tragedy. The next step is to advance a more accurate assessment of the situation in Southeast Asia that can lead to workable policies to implement the deep desire of many Americans to help improve the lot of the Vietnamese and other peoples of the area.

What are the basic foreign interests of the United States? Beyond our interest in assuring that no other nation can, or is highly tempted to, attack the United States itself (which probably still requires that neither the Soviet Union nor China gain control of the military potential of Western Europe or Japan), the basic foreign interests of the United States are only those which an overwhelming majority of the people of this country value so highly as to be willing to pay for them dearly out of national resources and energies that would otherwise go for domestic needs.

Our commitments to South Vietnam have never been subjected to this test of overwhelming popular support. Rather, U.S. administrations have heavily involved their own prestige—domestically and internationally—in these commitments, and have tried to set up an equation between the nation's interest and their own prestige. It must be admitted that an insufficiently vigilant Congress and an insufficiently informed public allowed this unfortunate false equation to take hold. Some segments of the Congress and the electorate were beguiled into believing that U.S. security was at stake in Southeast Asia. Others believed we were there for altruistic reasons—to aid economic and political development, or simply to prevent aggression. In fact, the connections between any outcomes of the Indo-china conflict and the security of the United States are tenuous at best; and the altruistic motives of our involvement, however real, are contradicted by the practical effects of our actions. Any American administration that

wants to reduce the damage to the international credit of
essential U.S. foreign undertakings, which will inevitably
accompany our pull-out from Vietnam, will have to deflate
the excessively expanded scope of our commitments and
to divest the United States of those commitments derived
from a superficial security rationale or a misapplied moral
concern.

But what happens to the nations of Southeast Asia? Can
we, once we have made them dependent on our assistance,
leave them to be gobbled up by "International Communism"? A realistic assessment of trends in Southeast
Asia should give weight to the nationalistic content of the
Vietnamese Communist movement—North and South—
and its function as a deterrent to any attempt by either
Russia or China to add Southeast Asia to their sphere of
control. Neither the Soviets nor the Chinese, especially as
their energies are absorbed in their rivalry with one
another, could afford to alienate the Vietnamese Communists, nor could they afford to get bogged down physically in Southeast Asia for any other reason.

Then what about the regime that governs Vietnam?
Are we now indifferent to the undemocratic aspects of
Communist systems? The political institutions through
which Vietnam is governed after the war, whatever the
ideological coloration of the regime, are likely to depart
drastically from our preferred Anglo-American models.
But only a fatuous moralist would insist on a non-Communist pattern at this stage in the socio-economic development of the country. Nor is there any reason to expect
that a Communist regime would do worse in developing
the country economically.

In sum, there is no compelling threat posed by an all-
Communist Vietnam to U.S. strategic/geopolitical interests or to our moral interests. A consolidation of Communist rule throughout Vietnam, then, need only be
considered a defeat of those U.S. objectives derived from

commitments which are themselves derived from flimsy geopolitical notions and naïve altruism.

Paradoxically, the war in Vietnam leaves the victor (Vietnam) in a physically devastated condition, while the vanquished (the United States) emerges intact, despite the loss of more than fifty thousand men, expenditure of well over $100 billion, and some accounts payable to deferred domestic needs, plus some bitter political divisions.

In such a situation, with the defeated nation better off economically than the victor, where is a refurbishment of U.S. international prestige to be sought? Certainly not in a sulking withdrawal from active concern for the future of Southeast Asia any more than in a quixotic attempt to build new counter-insurgency Maginot lines in Thailand or Malaysia.

There is a constructive opportunity here which, in a period of national self-flagellation, we might miss. The admiration the United States gained after World War II for its imaginative reconstruction policies benefiting former ally and opponent alike might be retrieved in the present context if this time we supported the reconstruction of the nation that defeated us. There are various ways this can be done. Prime Minister Palme of Sweden has urged the immediate establishment of an international organization to plan postwar aid to all of Vietnam. This might be the vehicle for reviving the American government's 1965 proposal for the developed nations to fund a Southeast Asian regional-development effort that would include North Vietnam. If we are prepared to make major contributions to such a program, agreeing to devolve the major planning and management responsibilities to international agencies, we may yet have a chance to decontaminate our foreign-assistance efforts from the anti-Communist virus. But this will require greater restraint, in action as well as rhetoric, than the fanfare surrounding the 1965 U.S. proposal. Our role should be restricted to

funding and only such technical assistance asked for by
the international agencies directing the program. Otherwise it will tend to be confused with the multilateral
regional-security efforts we have been championing as sub-
stitutes for a direct U.S. military presence.

Action along these lines banks on an uncharacteristic
humility in the U.S. policy community toward the past
and toward our future foreign interests. But such a reorientation is needed to transform what could otherwise be
an international disaster for this country into a period of
renewed international responsibility worthy of our best
traditions.

It is not enough to carp at our national leaders from
the sidelines for a mistaken involvement that proceeded
from a world-view most of us failed to oppose just a few
years ago. We must demand a reorientation; but we must
also assume the burden of devising alternatives that ask
for more than a national cop-out. Anything less is maso-
chism of the worst order.

VINTAGE POLITICAL SCIENCE
AND SOCIAL CRITICISM

VINTAGE BIOGRAPHY AND AUTOBIOGRAPHY

A free catalogue of VINTAGE BOOKS *will be sent at your request. Write to* Vintage Books, 457 Madison Avenue, New York, New York 10022.